ESSEX GOLD

"A Farm of four acres, if well handled, may give occupation, and even bring pecuniary gain, to the possessor. A garden for those who thoroughly understand and enjoy it may secure untold pleasures, and perhaps help to pay for the rent of the cottage. But an "oyster bed" is a pleasure – an el dorado – a mine of wealth, in fact, which fills the owners pockets with gold, and affords to the millions untold gastronomical enjoyment and healthy food."

John R Philpots
'Oysters and all about them' (1891)

End papers based on etchings of oyster dredgers by Arthur Briscoe

ESSEX GOLD

The fortunes of the Essex Oysterman

HERVEY BENHAM
in collaboration with Peter French
and John Leather

*Hervey Benham's Mersea
Smack Charlotte racing in
the Town Regatta, 1939*

Essex Record Office
Chelmsford 1993

ISBN 0 900360 92 5

A catalogue record for this book is available
from the British Library

Essex Record Office Publication No. 120

Designed and produced by Keith Mirams MCSD

Printed in England by
Lavenham Press Limited

Foreword

The death of Hervey Benham in 1987 deprived lovers of Essex coastal waters of a historian whose books have been a source of pleasure to this generation and will continue to be enjoyed by many more to come.

I had the privilege of knowing Hervey from my youth and benefited from his friendship in many ways. His qualities are too many to list. He was a man who had a great capacity for understanding the difficulties and problems of others. The advice he gave was always sound and calculated – quite often tersely and colourfully expressed but always with your well-being at heart. He could have been rightly proud of his many successes in the world of local newspapers and journalism, but from my intimate knowledge of him I would say his chief pride and pleasure was in exploring and recording local maritime history.

It was with great delight that I accepted his invitation to join with him in the production of a book on the history of the Essex oyster industry, a book, incidentally, which I tried to get him to write a long while ago. The period of a year and a half spent collecting the material with him was a very rewarding time for me. It altered many of my misconceptions about an industry with which I grew up. I am probably the sixth or seventh generation of my family to cultivate Essex oyster grounds.

Sadly when Hervey had almost completed his writing, it became apparent that the illness he had been resolutely fighting was beating him. He realised he was going to be unable to complete the final stages of preparing the work for publication, so he handed it all over to myself and John Leather (a well known marine historian in his own right) to prepare it for publication with instructions as to illustrations, John being well versed in this task.

Much more material has come to light since this was entrusted to us, but we have sought to keep faithfully to Hervey's text.

This is the last book from the pen of Hervey Benham, an account of the East Coast's greatest industry from our greatest writer on Essex maritime history. If readers glean some understanding and have some hours of enjoyment as they peruse its pages I know that would have been satisfaction enough for Hervey.

Peter R. French

Acknowledgements

This book owes much to the many people who gave their time and knowledge to enable this record to be made. Sadly we do not know the names of all of those who helped Hervey Benham and omissions are therefore inevitable. Thanks must go to Burge Everit of Brightlingsea, Tim Bell, Bob Cole of Burnham, Christopher Kerrison of the Colchester Oyster Fishery, Harry Banks of West Mersea, Ted Pitt of Maldon, Norman Childs and Mr Alf Pyner, historian of Burnham.

Mrs Margaret Pinkerton kindly allowed free and generous access to the family archives of the Wiseman family of Paglesham, now in her possession. Mark and Rosemary Roberts supplied information and permitted quotations from Rosemary's book on Paglesham.

Many of the illustrations are from Hervey Benham's collection, others are from my own and other private collections or from the Colchester and Essex Museum.

The Essex Record Office gave access to the wealth of records held there. In particular, the County Archivist, Victor Gray, lent help and enthusiasm without which this book would not have been published. Mrs Doris Redhouse patiently typed the text which enabled Hervey's text to be brought to print. Finally gratitude is due to Mrs Barbara Benham for her enthusiasm and great patience during the long time it has taken to get this unique record printed and available to the reader.

Peter R. French

Preface

This book is the result of a collaboration with a friend from boyhood days, Peter French, whose family have been oyster cultivators at West Mersea for over 150 years, and who himself is among the last to carry on the tradition there today. One of his ancestors, the James French mentioned among the laying-holders of 1825, was, according to family tradition, lost overboard about 1846 sailing a freight of oysters to Burnham in his smack Ellen and both Peter's sons became successful inshore fishermen with their own boats, though regrettably that calling now only provides a livelihood for one of them.

At the age of 14 Peter saved up to buy his first wash of oysters and was given a corner of his father's laying to tend them till he could sell them to the Whitstable boat. (Similarly Harry Banks, another old friend who has contributed to these pages, was initiated to the trade with a gift of 500 'Ports' while still a schoolboy.) Peter signed the old-fashioned forms of apprenticeship to his father, to give him the right to take his turn working for the Tollesbury and Mersea Oyster Company, though in fact he never availed himself of this, preferring to find an occupation more rewarding than that meagre livelihood. This was also the view of his father, Cassell French, for many years my neighbour and mentor, who also preferred to pass his turn with the company unless it also involved a remuneration for his smack, *Mersea Lass*.

The *Mersea Lass* must have wondered what had happened to her when Peter's turn came to take her over for, after half a century of gentle jogging about the Mersea oyster grounds, she was put to work on all kinds of inshore fishing, her little Handybilly auxiliary transferred to Cassell's converted lifeboat *Dolphin*, to be replaced by the biggest diesel she could carry. I recall one of the happiest weeks of my life spent inshore herring drifting with her out of Lowestoft. When this strenuous life at last proved too much for her old bones, Peter replaced the *Mersea Lass* with a succession of fishing boats more suited to the North Sea, working sometimes out of Boston and sometimes from North Shields. He never entirely deserted his oyster grounds, however, and ultimately this way of life, which in younger years had seemed too dull and unadventurous, attracted him back to cultivate the family layings in the Strood Channel, some ground in Tollesbury Creek and for a while a hired laying in the Crouch. This was not a usual career, rather surprisingly, for fishing would seem ideal for youth and oystering for maturer years, yet few Essex men followed this pattern. Most were lifelong fishermen or oystermen.

This book ends with the story of Peter's ill-fated venture into artificial nursery breeding, but I am glad to record that despite annual protestations of retirement, he still succeeds in finding supplies to re-lay in Tollesbury Creek and so is likely to be the last man able to claim 50 years continuous production.

The technical sections of this book have thus been largely at Peter's dictation. My own fascination with the old pound-a-week world of lost content goes back well over half a century, but only as observer and occasional amateur participant. While my young friends hankered to be crewing in a yacht race, I delighted to spend holidays dredging for 'the Company' with dear kindly Charlie Hewes and merry, sharp-tongued 'Sooty' Mussett, either in Charlie's smack *Charlotte,* which I later acquired for a yacht, proud to have her recognised by the Dutch fishermen in Willemstadt as 'oude English oostersmak', or in 'Sooty's' boat, which being smaller was better suited for Thornfleet Creek. Hour after hour Charlie would work her up that narrow channel, from Deeps to the Gut, hove-to across the tide, somehow missing the yachts and their moorings (which of course were then much more widely spaced), hardly touching the tiller, but all the time rucking down the peak of the mainsail to let her drop astern, setting it up to make her drive ahead. As we reached the Gut and picked up the last dredge, 'Sooty' would observe, "Goo on Charles. Oi've had enough of this, let's have a good sail down to the Bench Head." And Charlie would growl, "Don't talk so daft, Soot. Set yer foresail and shet up".

Thirty years later when such arts were forgotten in Essex, I made the acquaintance of two Restronguet dredgermen, Frank Cock and Harry Barnes, and found it all still going on in the Fal. Dredging with them in Frank's *Morning Star* brought back all the peace and calm of the Mersea of my boyhood, for by common consent motors have never been allowed to be used on the Truro oyster grounds, which remain to this day the only fishery in the world worked under sail. The tranquillity of a world where no machinery stirs needs to be experienced to be believed; once again I was listening to conversations between boats carried on, not on the crackling, chattering radio, but directly across a hundred yards of water, with voices hardly raised, even if the topic now was likely to be the quality of the previous evening's T.V. programmes.

As to published material, I have relied for general background largely on the admirable article in the *Victoria County History of Essex* (Vol. II) and on John Philpot's *Oysters and All About Them,* a two-volume dog's dinner published in 1891 and quoting many of the reports by Board of Trade inspectors produced around this time. Where I have not specified a source in a footnote, references to this period are mostly from Philpots or the Local Government Board reports on cholera, particularly that by Dr Bulstrode in 1896. I have read innumerable other books and articles on the subject, for the capacity of the oyster to arouse popular curiosity has long extended to provoking amateur experts into picking up their pens, and indeed still exerts its spell on the editors of Sunday magazine supplements and the producers of television features. The volume of this material, however, so much exceeds its value that I have not burdened these pages with a conventional bibliography, but would refer the reader to my references, which include the sources I have found useful.

Most of the local material I have found in the Essex Record Office, and in the Local Studies Department of the Colchester Public Library, where my thanks are due to many members of the staff for endless patient help. I am also grateful to Doris Redhouse of West Mersea for two years of tireless typing.

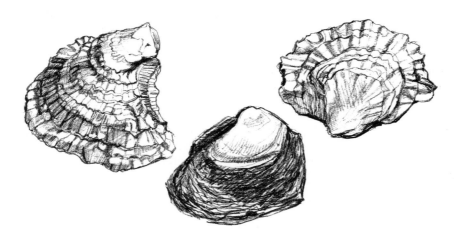

Native oysters

Contents

Introduction

The placid oyster, unchanging in his own habits, has undergone many and varied fluctuations of fortune from the times when he was freely and universally available for the taking, through periods when the teeming populations of ill-fed cities depended on him for a succulent item of diet, through others when he was the ultimate delight of the sophisticated gourmet, till his own popularity has brought him close to extinction. He has been cared for and neglected, farmed and fought over, he has been both poisoned and poisoner, but he has never been out of favour or fashion.

In this book I have tried to picture the place of the oyster in Essex life and history. Before exploring this strange and little-known world, however, it may be well to attempt a general summary and to touch in a little of the background to the events and practices described in later chapters.

Shells of the English native oyster have been found in the kitchen rubbish of ancient British homes and Roman villas – even in Imperial Rome itself. The grounds on which they grew reflect the story of English land tenure, for while some remained common, most were bestowed by Royal grant on manors and municipal corporations. Their cultivators have evolved down the centuries from serfs and villeins into licensed dredgermen or copyhold tenants, with freehold ownership becoming common only in the last hundred years.

Oyster fisheries were not sufficiently important, or more probably sufficiently defined, to attract the attention of the Domesday census-takers.[1] Colchester's rights over the Colne may be traced back to the 11th century, and the charter granting them has become closely associated with the oyster fishery, where its reading is part of the annual opening ceremony.

The medieval town made what profit it could from selling licences to dredge and monopolising the sales outlets, but an organised fishery with systematic routines of cultivation was probably not established until the 18th century. Before this time rules and orders everywhere were chiefly directed to controlling abuse and over-exploitation, the most conspicuous being the oyster byelaws enacted in 1697 by the Company of Free Fishermen covering the Thames Estuary between London Bridge, Harwich and the North Foreland, and including waters, rivers, creeks and places 'within the bounds of the said Charter'. Some 17 ordinances restricted fishing at certain times and places, laid down penalties for encroachments on layings, and forbade dredging in any river, creek or fleet which did not naturally stock itself, unless with the permission of the Company. Apprenticeship to a freeman for seven years was also made compulsory, but there is no means of telling if these rules were honoured in the breach or the observance.[2]

A century later more positive policies were emerging, as in response to the growing demand the traditional controlled gathering in of uncultured oysters gave way to a sophisticated form of specialist husbandry, with oysters spatting on ground selected and 'culched' to receive them, nursed and protected for four or five years, and finally fattened for market on other ground favoured for this purpose. Burnham and the Crouch may well have led the way in this direction, for its 'wallfleets' were acclaimed above all others in the 16th century, though for the past three hundred years the pre-eminence of the Colchester native has been generally recognised.

The little tenanted oyster farms or layings had also by the 17th century established the pattern which lasted till recent times, with each man concerned to cultivate his own patch and replenish it from common ground in the neighbourhood, developing that long, patient, year-by-year intercourse with nature which was the essence of true oyster cultivation, involving as it did a long cycle of carefully nurtured development from spat through half-ware and ware into brood and finally the mature oyster.

There were, however, other aspects. The deep-sea trade was a hard and hazardous calling far removed from the peaceful life of the husbandmen of the creeks and estuaries. As a result of changing tastes and conditions, 'deep-seas' have now disappeared to such an extent that it would be difficult to find anybody who has seen one, let alone tasted it.

Buying and selling also became increasingly important by the end of the 17th century, for, unlike the farmer ashore, reaping at harvest time the crop he had sown the previous spring or autumn, the oysterman's spatfall was erratic, with perhaps one bounteous gift of nature in five lean years, so most laying-holders spent some of their earnings on sustaining their stocks, and in bumper years supplemented those earnings by disposing of their own surplus. A few smallholders continued to the end to be content with disposing of whatever nature provided, but in the 18th century the larger growers – and many of the not so large – came to regard and describe themselves as oyster merchants – a parallel with the country millers who, after centuries of grinding bespoke lots of grain from fields within a few miles of the mill, found themselves during the same period visiting Mark Lane to expend their own capital on the raw material to feed their stones.

Native oyster cultivation reached its peak in the mid-19th century, certainly as far as the East Coast was concerned.

The boom came with phenomenal spatfalls in 1857, 1858 and 1859, after four bad years. These harvests were coming on the market in 1862 when the wholesale price dropped to two guineas a bushel, or 2s. 6d. a hundred, so that retailers were charging only sixpence or eightpence a dozen.[3]

This was the time which prompted Sam Weller's observation in *Pickwick Papers*: "It's a wery remarkable circumstance that poverty and oysters always seem to go together." According to one estimate in 1864, the working classes and labourers of London annually spent £125,000 on 124 million

Oyster smacks and peter boats discharging at London's Billingsgate fish market in the early 19th century.

oysters at four a penny, a total exceeded only by the expenditure on cockles, mussels, whelks, winkles and shrimps.[4]

Nature could not sustain such a turnover. With spatfalls returning to normal, the price rose in 1863 to four guineas a bushel. By 1889 it touched £16 a bushel, or half-a-crown a dozen. While renewed spatfalls brought some reductions, the oyster had ceased to be the poor man's staple and established itself as the rich man's delicacy.

The seller's market suited the merchants. Indeed, one thing an oysterman always feared as much as a shortage, when he had nothing to sell, was a glut, when he could not sell it; any inquiry as to the state of his affairs invariably found him pessimistically predicting the dire effects of one or the other. In 1885 the Rector of Brightlingsea, Canon Arthur Pertwee, noted 'a considerable difference in the oyster market from last year. Once more there is the promise, or the threat, of what the British public had despaired of ever seeing again – a cheap oyster'.

So far as native oysters were concerned the promise was never to be fulfilled. The government intervened with legislation to promote the formation of limited liability companies, resulting in the enclosure of common grounds in the Blackwater and Roach, but the Victorian faith in capital and business management failed to live up to its promise. Production never again reached the levels of the 1860s, and to satisfy the continuing demand the merchants turned increasingly to relaying foreign oysters.

Imports from western France, referred to as 'Brittanies' were common in

Essex back into the seventeenth century. These, being flat native oysters of the same species *(ostrea edulis),* not only increased home turnover, but also spatted on local grounds and so helped to sustain stocks at the level necessary for the cycle of survival.

As the demand increased, other foreign imports became of increasing importance, and established a quite different sort of cultivation, for in most cases these were bought half-grown and laid on the Essex grounds in spring for fattening and sale the following winter. Some would be kept in wintering pits for a second season's growth, but in general there was no long careful cultivation of the kind required for the natives.

Portuguese oysters *(ostrea angulata)* and American Bluepoints were already being laid in large numbers in Brightlingsea Creek (and doubtless elsewhere) during the second half of the nineteenth century. Which came first, and when, is unrecorded, but it seems likely that both were in demand to meet the insatiable market after native spatfalls could no longer sustain the record consumption of the 1850s. While the Bluepoints never attained wide popularity, the 'Ports' played an increasingly important role in the smaller operators' economy and did come close to re-establishing the 'cheap oyster' in popular favour in the 1930s, till they in turn succumbed to diseases in their native Tagus River, and were replaced by an oyster of Pacific origin, the Gigas.

The Bluepoints were a species akin to the natives, flat shelled but coarser and rougher, and capable of spatting on Essex grounds, though to what extent they did so is not clear. The knobbly, round-shelled Portuguese and Gigas oysters on the other hand, seldom spatted in the cold northern waters, and had to be replaced as they were sold.

Since they were less prone to be 'sick' during the spatting season, they could be marketed in summer, a great advantage for the growers' annual cash flow. The merchant based his trade on selling for roughly twice the price he paid, which, allowing for a mortality of up to ten per cent, would cover the costs of his investment and labour.

The foreign imports preserved many fisheries which would otherwise have gone to the wall, but they brought new problems with them in the way of foreign pests, notably the American tingle which from the late nineteenth century onwards became one of the most destructive enemies the oysterman had to face, and the slipper limpet, which appeared around 1912 and from that time on required endless labour and effort to prevent it smothering once fertile grounds.

The increasing populations which provided such vast markets also produced new problems of pollution from sewage, with the oyster for the first time recognised as a health hazard.

A Local Government Board report on the alarming cholera outbreak of 1893[5] pointed the finger of suspicion, and another report by Dr. Bulstrode, 'On Oyster Cultivation in Relation to Disease', published in 1896, was devastating. It identified four places where pits and layings were exposed to sewage outfalls.

At Southend layings to the east of the pier were passed as safe but ground to the west of it was condemned, with the result that cultivation here came to an end. At nearby Leigh, Hadleigh Ray was also suspect, especially on the flood tide, but the Kent and Essex Sea Fisheries Committee, showing all the complacency to be expected from an association of vested interests, protested that the shore to the west of Leigh was unpopulated, save for South Benfleet where there was drainage from a mere fifteen houses. At Brightlingsea cement-lined pits beside the Hard, full of native and foreign oysters, were dangerously close to sewage outfalls. The merchants protested, with logic but without avail, that 'the sewage was brought to them and not their seeking'. Even the Sea Fisheries Committee found the place deserving of censure. Wivenhoe, by this time declining in importance as a centre, still had two pits on the foreshore. William Bartlett replaced his with a new one dug on the opposite side of the river. The other owner, Mr. Heath, planned a 'floating ledging', to receive water only on the flood tide and to close on the ebb, but soon he too bought a bit of ground on the Fingringhoe shore. At West Mersea an offensive pit close to the Victory Inn was filled in. This was the old Victory at the bottom of The Lane, beside which ran a stream elegantly known as The Bumby, carrying the effluent from the cottages' privies.

The whole affair was invariably referred to in the trade as 'the oyster scare' and dismissed with derisive indignation. But public confidence was badly shaken and any hope of sweeping 'the scare' under the carpet was dashed by an outbreak of typhoid in 1902 following a mayoral banquet at Winchester and a corporation banquet the following day at Southampton, with Emsworth oysters on both menus. Several people died, including the Dean of Winchester. The Worshipful Company of Fishmongers banned the sale of Emsworth oysters, and Essex Medical Officers of Health had to attend Fishmongers Hall to defend the precautions taken by them, with Dr. Dickin vouching that Brightlingsea oysters were now 'quite free of sewage contamination' and Mr. Sowden insisting there had 'never been an outbreak of typhoid from eating Colchester oysters'.

Fortunately most of the Essex grounds were remote from centres of population – one reason for the industry's survival – but there was further trouble at Brightlingsea around 1930 (by which time native oysters had been replaced by American Bluepoints and 'Ports'), solved by the building of a cleansing station, and in the late 1960s after further typhoid cases purification became compulsory at Mersea. Fortunately a cheap process based on the sterilisation of water by ultra-violet light was available to save what remained of the trade.

Finally nature seemed to conclude that if man wished to destroy his heritage by spreading pests in waters fouled by pollution she might as well finish the job. A mysterious mortality decimated stocks in 1920, and

*Washing oysters prior to
putting them through the
cleansing tank for
marketing.*

though it never struck so viciously again it recurred from year to year. It
was at first blamed on the dumping at sea of thousands of tons of T.N.T.
after the First World War, perhaps in the hope of claiming compensation,
but no connection was established. After patiently building up stocks, and
heavy investments in 'Ports', the diminishing number of growers survived
the Second World War only to see the fruits of their labours reduced to ruin
by the winter of 1945. A few tried yet again, only for the winter of 1962/3 to
wreak a still more complete havoc, which brought cultivation in the Colne
to a halt for the first time in a thousand years, caused the Roach River Company to throw in its hand, closed the ambitious purifying plant at
Brightlingsea and effectively brought oyster cultivation in Essex to an end.
One or two merchants struggled to make a new start with supplies from
areas less severely affected, but were never again rewarded with a worthwhile spatfall, perhaps because the oyster population had fallen below the
numbers necessary for survival, perhaps also because the creeks were now
poisoned by chemicals sprayed on the broad Essex acres around them, as
continues to this day, and still more by a lethal anti-fouling paint, T.B.T.,
used to kill growth on yachts' bottoms till it was made illegal in 1987.

A few of the more enterprising growers, however, found ways to extend
native cultivation for another twenty years. With the Blackwater spatting
grounds as well as the creek layings laid in ruins by the winter of 1962-3,
the only hope for those determined to try again was to look further afield,
and two new sources of supply, long neglected or forgotten, were discovered.

The West Country had escaped more lightly, and it was found that the Truro dredgermen, still quietly working the Corporation's ground under sail in their little half-deck cutters, sensibly limiting themselves to a six-month season and a six-hour day, were glad of a new market. Thus the old link with the Fal was restored, first by Peter French and then by Christopher Kerrison of the Colne Fishery, on a new and happier basis. Instead of the old buccaneering raids, some lasting friendships developed out of the trade between former adversaries.

In the 1960s another and more productive supply was discovered in the Solent, where well-stocked ground in Stanswood Bay, near Southampton, had been unaccountably overlooked. Probably the warm water from the nearby power station must be given credit for the survival and revival of this fishery. This time the approach was more traditional. In 1971 half-a-dozen boats from Mersea, Brightlingsea and Maldon dredged and brought home over a hundred tons from this newly discovered Klondyke. The old enmity flared up once again – the last example of many down the ages. The Essex men figured on local T.V. as 'East Coast pirates', and the following year the Solent fishermen obtained the protection of a Several Order despite the opposition of Colne Oyster Fishery, the Fishermen's Association of Maldon and Peter French. Supplies continued to be obtained for several years from all over the Solent, including Portsmouth Harbour, but competition from French buyers re-stocking their depleted fisheries sent prices soaring.

There were, however, still further troubles in store, in the shape of new diseases even more deadly than the mortality of the 1920s. These posed such a threat to the industry by the 1970s that the Ministry of Agriculture and Fisheries in 1974 introduced the Molluscan Shellfish (Control of Deposits) Order, which prohibited the movement of oysters from pest-ridden areas for re-laying in areas free of pests. It was subsequently invoked to ban imports from France, Spain and Portugal, in the hope of arresting the spread of Aber disease, which wreaked havoc throughout the French fisheries following its discovery at L'Aberwach in Brittany about 1967, and again as a defence against a parasitic disease, Bonamia, which appeared in France in the late 1970s, decimating stocks there, spreading through Holland to Denmark, and virtually wiping out the stocks of *ostrea edulis.* Only the Gravenhage Schelde escaped thanks to the prudent management of the Dutch government. Incomprehensibly – for there was no export of affected oysters – it also appeared in 1987 in New Zealand where the Foveaux Strait Fishery had to be closed.[6] This parasite infected the bloodstream of the oysters, which after six months or so died suddenly.

The order, which was probably not even known to some Customs officers in the smaller ports, was ineffective. In 1982 Bonamia was confirmed as the cause of heavy mortality in Mylor Creek in the Fal Estuary, from which source oysters had been re-laid in West Mersea beds in September of that year. Soon all the Mersea layings were stricken, and the disease was found in the Colne, Walton Backwaters and Paglesham.

Affected stocks had to be destroyed and grounds cleared to prevent re-infection. The Ministry then withdrew all movement licences, cutting off any possibility of re-stocking and effectively ordering the end of all cultivation. The oystermen sought compensation, quoting payments made to farmers for livestock compulsorily destroyed to counter foot-and-mouth disease, but the parallel was rejected. The Government maintained its age-old responsibility for the trade (based in the last half-century more on a sense of history than on its commercial importance in the national economy), but its solicitude, despite some previous grants for clearing limpets, did not in this crisis extend beyond regulation and restriction, backed by advisory and experimental services.

Finally, however, protests and objections were so strong that a concession was made, with the Ministry continuing to permit re-laying from 'clean' areas, of which the Solent was the most important. This enabled a few cultivators to carry on, but they could only re-lay for six to eight months, with oysters too small for sale then having to be destroyed to minimise risk of infection.

In 1986 Bonamia was discovered in the Solent. Alarmed at the probable loss of their home market and the possible destruction of their entire stocks, the dredgermen fished them out and exported them to Spain. Thus threatening last major source of supply, at home or overseas, to which the few surviving cultivators could look for survival, leaving only an occasional small windfall to appear in some forgotten South Coast corner, and to be snapped up at astronomical prices.

It may be that the native oyster will re-establish himself, though stocks everywhere have long fallen below the level needed for survival, let alone revival. It has been estimated that every spatting oyster may produce three-quarters of a million larvae, of which, however, less than one per cent will reach the stage of settling as spat, even in favourable seasons. Again only one per cent of these spat are likely to survive the first year, so the survival rate is no more than one hundredth of one per cent, under the best conditions. Against such odds it has been estimated that 100,000 oysters is the minimum stock with any prospect of establishing itself.[7]

No doubt natural disasters have in the past reduced Essex stocks below survival level, though it may be doubted that a previous quarter-century has passed without a significant spatfall. Up to, say, the First World War, the solution was to replenish them from elsewhere, by fair means or foul. The piratical raids on the ancient fisheries of Orford and Burnham, described in Chapter 13, were examples of the desperate measures adopted to remedy a mid-eighteenth century crisis which may perhaps have borne a resemblance to today's condition. But the more legitimate, though scarcely less provocative onslaught on the Solent's common grounds two hundred years later is unlikely to be repeated, for today the once numerous grounds around the coast of the British Isles are mostly abandoned and barren, with the few survivors closely protected.

A likelier solution may be found in the sort of artificial nursery production described in Chapter 18, which came within an ace of providing a population capable of subsequent natural regeneration. Nature may yet relent and smile once again on the East coast as she has recently done in the South. To this day a few natives stubbornly survive along the shore off Mersea Reach and in such unlikely places as the channels around the inhospitable Buxey Sand, keeping alive the last flicker of the old traditional 'outside' dredging, and providing a reminder that nature is inscrutable and that the oyster is a hardy survivor as well as a delicate and vulnerable customer. Despite this, any widespread reappearance of spat now seems beyond the most optimistic bounds of possibility, but nurseries could yet provide a new breeding stock and then 'top up' natural resources in the same way that these have in the past had to be supplemented by imports from other areas.

French fisheries, far more extensive than any in this country, have suffered comparable disasters and have found their answer in the growing of Pacific oysters known as Gigas, which have proved immune to Bonamia. These knobbly little oysters, unlike the native *edulis,* do not incubate their spawn within the female oyster, but release it direct into the sea where it is fertilised, though since water temperatures higher than those usually reached in this country are required it is unlikely to breed here. Nevertheless, commercial hatcheries are successfully producing its spat, and it already satisfies some of the 'popular' market once dominated by 'Ports'. This market is, however, much more important in France, with its big domestic consumption, than in this country, where for a century the demand has been for a high-quality delicacy. Attempts to introduce Gigas at Mersea did not succeed, as described in Chapters 17 and 18; they might yet meet with better success, but today the limited demand is fully supplied. A flat-shelled oyster immune to Bonamia, *ostrea virginica*, has also be re-introduced in small numbers for an experimental breeding stock, but this like the 'Ports' is only another summer oyster and so can be no substitute for the true native.

Thus, though many good oyster grounds remain, despite the loss of many creeks for yacht moorings, or their destruction by silting and tidal erosion, traditions have been so shattered, and any new techniques are likely to be so revolutionary, that it may be too much to hope that Essex will again re-establish itself as the stronghold of the trade it has so long dominated.

This book is concerned with the oyster fisheries of Essex. It must, however, be remembered that up to little more than a century ago oyster cultivation was nationwide, extending round the shores of the British Isles, with fisheries great and small flourishing in innumerable creeks and estuaries and even on open foreshores and offshore sandbanks. The extent of the trade gave it strength, for one area affected by poor spatfalls could sustain its stock from elsewhere, while some fisheries were always natural spatting grounds and others better for fattening. Burnham must have largely depended on supplies from the Channel Islands at the end of the eighteenth century, and other trading links with fisheries down Channel and around the coast from the Forth to the Solway are described in a later chapter.

Outside the Thames estuary, with some notable exceptions including Cornwall and the Solent, most of these fisheries declined into extinction in the nineteenth century[8] as a result of industrial and sewage pollution, neglect or over-fishing both locally and by 'foreign' raiders, chiefly from Essex. It is not too much to say that the survival and growth of the Essex industry was largely based on the destruction of its competitors. The Queen's Bench was called on in 1814 to decide if a Colchester fisherman named Richardson was justified in taking brood from Chichester Harbour, and ruled in his favour because he was preserving it, not destroying it. As a result the Colneside marauders considered they had the right to strip any common grounds they could reach.

Thus by the end of the nineteenth century oyster cultivation was chiefly based in the Thames estuary. The Essex estuaries and creeks and the Whitstable flats had been spared the worst effects of pollution, and they were advantageously placed for the great metropolitan market when so many millions of oysters were sailed direct to Billingsgate. Moreover, Essex and Kent, old enemies in many matters maritime, complemented each other for oyster production, and in fact formed one huge natural fishery, with Essex producing so much spat and brood and the wide Kentish flats so ideal to mature it into perfect oysters. Hence a great part of the Essex trade came to depend on supplying Kent, with the Whitstable companies retaining a buyer at Brightlingsea and sending their smacks to collect weekly from Burnham and Mersea. So much did Whitstable come to rely on Essex that by 1900 the Kentish flatsmen could not get a living dredging on their own common ground, for the local companies preferred to buy the quantity and quality they required from Essex rather than rely on the casual catching of their own dredgermen. Indeed, among the Essex growers, the Colne oyster fishery was probably the only one to retain its independence of Whitstable and sustain itself as a self-sufficient business.

So dominant did the Thames Estuary become that in 1879 Dr. Frank Buckland defined a 'native' oyster as one taken inside a line drawn from Harwich to Margate.[9] This led the *Victoria County History of Essex* to declare: 'The term "native" is sometimes applied to any oyster bred in the United Kingdom; but strictly it should be applicable only to oysters bred in Essex and Kent. In this counties, the chief English oyster spatting estuaries are found, and here alone, says Buckland, the oyster is truly "native", it being introduced and cultivated elsewhere.

It is difficult to follow or accept this argument, which has been widely published, causing much confusion and misunderstanding. Countless places around the coast, as has been mentioned, produced their own natives; indeed if the argument is to be carried to its ultimate conclusion it

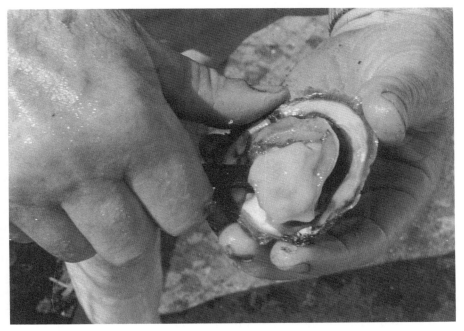

Gourmets' Delight: a fat oyster opened ready for immediate consumption.

may be contended that there were few, if any, Whitstable natives during the last half century of that fishery's existence.

In the following chapters I have been able to refer to fisheries elsewhere only where they impinge directly on the Essex story, but the Kentish link is so close – half rivalry, half partnership – that Whitstable must be briefly mentioned here, along with a few others.

The Whitstable smacks worked down Channel, as the Essex men did. The Whitstable Company advertised in the *Kentish Gazette* in 1769, offering £1 16s per wash for oysters brought from Shoreham, Portsmouth and Poole, and numerous voyages are recorded in 1784-5 to Falmouth, Portsmouth and Cancale in Brittany. In the mid-nineteenth century about twenty smacks are remembered to have sailed annually to the Channel Islands for brood, and in 1875 Henry Gann of the Seasalter and Ham Company built the big smack *Seasalter* as a carrier, with a load-line on her side.

But the Kentish men do not seem to have hunted as much and as far afield as the Essex men did. Whenever there was a good spatfall on the Whitstable flats, a few Colne smacks would join the local 'yawls', but there is neither record nor recollection of Whitstable or Rochester smacks seeking their fortune on the Essex common grounds, or on the East Coast generally. The explanation probably is that there were fewer private layings in Kent, so the brood market was largely in the hands of the companies who, as mentioned, found they could get better bargains from the Essex specialists.

The Whitstable Oyster Fishery Company derived from a Company of

Dredgers which from time immemorial enjoyed the right to dredge on grounds belonging to Whitstable Manor. In 1792 the marine port of the Manor was bought by Thomas Foord, who conveyed it to the Company of Dredgers, which was in the following year incorporated by Act of Parliament as 'The Company of Free Fishers and Dredgers of Whitstable'.

For a century the fishery was run by a foreman, deputy foreman, water bailiff and twelve jurymen, all elected annually. Eldest sons of freemen of the company were admitted at the age of sixteen, younger sons and the sons of strangers at the age of twenty-one after a seven-year apprenticeship, but as this produced an excessive membership only eldest sons were enrolled at the age of twenty-one after 1881. Plans for more conventional capitalists to buy out the members' interests obtained Parliamentary approval in 1896, but the funds were not forthcoming, and the old company was left in possession of the Act, which fixed the nominal capital of the public company at £250,000. Each member was allotted twenty £10 shares, with the same apportionment to enrolled sons of members, and a life interest in seven £10 shares to each widow. The fishery was said to employ twenty-two boats in 1734, upwards of seventy in 1790 and about eighty in 1902.[10]

The Herne Bay, Hampton and Reculver Oyster Fishery Company was one of the notable failures among the many established at this time. It was set up by Act of Parliament passed in 1864, with a capital of £100,000 and powers to borrow a further £250,000. Frank Buckland, then an Inspector of Fisheries, was one of the directors. By 1874 it was inoperative due, in the charitable opinion of another Inspector, S. Walpole, 'rather to a want of means than of will; in other words, the company was rather unfortunate than in fault'.

Elsewhere in Kent it would be interesting to compare the Corporation of Rochester's control over the Medway with Colchester's over the Colne. An Act of 1729 confirmed Rochester's rights from 'time out of mind', but by the end of the nineteenth century the only layings in the Medway were at Ham Ooze, Colemouth Creek, Sharfleet and Stangate Creek.

Norfolk too invites comparisons. The Lynn Deeps fishery in the Wash was divided so that one-third was under the joint control of King's Lynn and Boston corporations, each appointing its own water bailiff, and the remaining two-thirds was controlled by King's Lynn. A Government report in 1876, observing that the fishery had been prosperous thirty years previously, but was then in decay, noted that under the joint arrangement nothing at all had been done. King's Lynn had closed its grounds for three years in 1872, but as soon as they were re-opened they were cleaned out in three months, 696,000 oysters being taken – an event which gave a bad name to the policy of compulsory closures, and was often quoted as an argument against them. The Lynn men preferred their more constant and reliable mussel fishery which lay to the south of the oyster grounds, and was twice as valuable in the 1870s. In 1871, of 125 boats at work, only two were oystering, and when as many as a hundred were counted on the oyster grounds less than a dozen were from Lynn. The techniques of oyster and mussel cultivation would make another intriguing study, with the mussels worked from scaups to lays just as the oysters were from off-shore and estuary grounds on to layings. Elsewhere in Norfolk there were in 1895 pits and layings, chiefly used for mussels but often for oysters also, at Blakeney, Overy Staithe, Brancaster Staithe and Wells. Even in neighbouring Suffolk I have touched only on the Orwell, the Stour and the Alde, though in the Deben there were layings up to six miles below Woodbridge, with the chief cultivation below Ramsholt, using pits below the ferry.

These and many other associated subjects must be left for others to study and describe. The Essex story is enough, for it deals with what has been justly called 'one of the oldest industries we possess, and quite the most interesting and most distinctive, fore in no othere county has it been carried on so long and to the same extent'.

It was a livelihood uniquely combining farming and fishing, a beautiful and characterful calling, basically bucolic, but often quarrelsome and occasionally adventurous, full of its own lore, traditions and mystique, always baffling and mysterious even to those who gave their lifetimes to it. There was no other occupation like it, and there never will be anything of the sort again, for though means will no doubt be found of satisfying the eternal and insatiable appetite for the most subtle and succulent of all gastronomic delicacies, the old mysteries, techniques and traditions, the accumulation of two thousand years' experience and endeavour, have passed away beyond recall in our lifetime.

Mechanical handling of oyster dredges speeds and eases the work of the fishery.

13

The dredgerman's art

The state of the oyster world at the dawn of history is anybody's guess. Judging by the enormous deposits of shells found at so many places there was no scarcity. It is also a fair surmise that the earliest oyster gatherers, including the proverbial brave man who was the first to swallow one, were content to pick them up where they lay – and that it was not long before someone devised a primitive dredge to make this task easier and to reach ground below low water mark. Just when that implement evolved into its modern form is another guess, but a medieval dredge would probably be recognisable, and usable, today.

The design of this implement – a triangular iron frame rigged with a bag into which anything on the sea bed is swept by a hoe-like scraper, called the scythe in Essex and the blade in Cornwall – varies little in basic form throughout the country, and probably evolved out of some primitive wooden frame and net dragged through the water by its owner. In that case it may share a common ancestry with the beam trawl, which for centuries, as the medieval 'wunderthon' and the later Leigh 'trimtram', also relied on a bottom scraper board, before someone had the idea of hanging

Some traditional tools of the the oysterman : left to right, a laying 'tendle' basket, baskets for packing oysters for despatch to market, an 'evil' or prong for lifting oysters, 'cultacs' for sorting and separating oysters and, behind, a hand dredge.

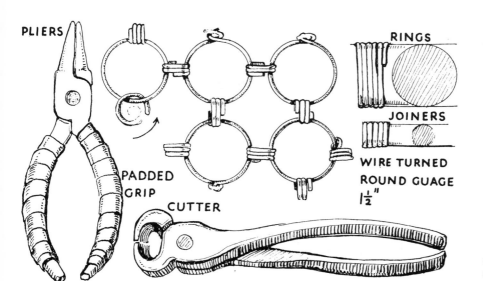

PLIERS

RINGS

JOINERS

WIRE TURNED
ROUND GUAGE
$1\frac{1}{2}$"

PADDED
GRIP

CUTTER

Chain mesh for the belly of a traditional oyster dredge.

the net from a beam raised on iron runner heads. The 'trimtram' shrimp trawl retained its triangular wooden frame till it was discarded within living memory.

The scythe on a hand dredge was from two to three feet long and attached to it was a bottom net made of wire rings. The upper part of the bag was netted from hambro line or similar twine, and was laced to a cross-member about halfway down the legs of the triangle. Where the two nets met they were secured to a wooden bar called the chapstick; Maldon and Tollesbury dredges also rigged wooden members along each side of the join, called 'dolly legs', which were considered to make the dredge less liable to turn over on its back, and also allowed the twine top to be rigged slacker than the wire bottom. The wire netting bellies were made by twisting the wire into rings around a pole about 1½ inches in diameter, and joining them with small rings called 'shuts' made on round-nosed pliers. Making 'riggings', as the wire bottoms were called, provided an occupation for a few old dredgermen. At Tollesbury after the men had gone ashore, one such (perhaps the watchman) would settle down on deck to spend the rest of the day making rings, like a woman at her knitting. 'Riggings' could be ordered with rings of various sizes, specified by the number of rings across; for whelking small rings were required. When oyster dredges were used for collecting 'five-fingers', thus converting a dreaded pest into a useful agricultural fertiliser, the netting was slacked back off the frame to increase capacity, and the scraper was sometimes 'wolded' with old rope, as its hoeing effect was not required.

The wire netting rigging, however, only came into use around the mid-nineteenth century. Earlier dredges had a bottom consisting of a piece of hide, with long slits in it to let some of the mud escape[1]. This was considered kinder on delicate brood, which were less scraped and scratched, though the wire rings had the advantage that they let the small stuff fall through. 'Half-skin-backed' dredges were used in the Blackwater in the 1880s, that is, with hide on the scraper and wire rings between this and the chapstick, but it is not clear whether this was a transitional development, or a form specially kept for brood dredging.[2] To this day old Maldon dredgermen refer to wire riggings as 'ring hides' – a curious terminological confusion.

The crossbar was traditionally not welded or rivetted to the side members, but was hammered thin and wrapped around them. In recent years, the few new dredges made have usually been welded, sometimes with a piece of chain link fencing laced in to save the labour of ring-making, and one or two have been seen with stainless steel riggings. Even after hide was abandoned for riggings, it was still used to cut lacings to fix the net to its frame, till this material was abandoned in favour of strips cut from inner tubes of car tyres, which lasted longer, and indeed often outlasted the iron frames to which the net was laced.

Hand dredges were about five feet long and at Mersea and Maldon weighed 18 or 20lbs, with Tollesbury favouring 22lbs, though they become lighter with age. The blacksmith set the edge of the 'hoe' so that when it lay flat on the ground the ring was about knee height, though some fussy customers required it to touch the thigh or the upper calf of the leg. Deep sea dredges were of basically similar design but with scrapers up to six feet long. After the Second World War the Ministry of Agriculture and Fisheries displayed a bureaucratic benevolence recalling the enthusiasm of the Board of Trade a century before, and attempted improved versions for

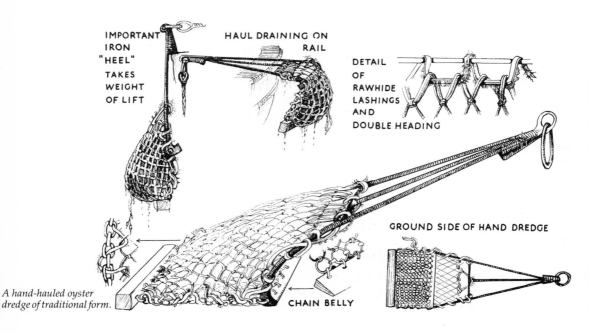

IMPORTANT IRON "HEEL" TAKES WEIGHT OF LIFT

HAUL DRAINING ON RAIL

DETAIL OF RAWHIDE LASHINGS AND DOUBLE HEADING

GROUND SIDE OF HAND DREDGE

CHAIN BELLY

A hand-hauled oyster dredge of traditional form.

Smacks dredging under sail in the Blackwater in the 1920s.

power craft, including a box dredge designed at their Conway Research Station which, however, never found much favour in Essex.

Dredging was primarily carried out under sail, and was an art in its own right. The smack had to drive with the tide, so the preferred conditions were a wind across the tide. The smack hove-to, with mainsail reefed, fore-sail aback, and a little 'spitfire' jib on the bowsprit. The dredges were cast over the weather rail, with the heaviest one forward and the lightest aft, because when the smack drove ahead the heaviest dredge required the shortest warp and the dredges thus kept clear of each other. (The fact that the skipper worked aft, and thus handled the lightest dredge, may also have had something to do with it.) Normally one man worked two dredges, but on the well-stocked parts of the Tollesbury and Mersea Company's grounds one dredge kept him busy, while on the clean sparsely populated sand of 'The Main' one man could work eight dredges, giving each twenty minutes between hauls. The dredge had to be thrown 'heel to tide', so that it entered the water with the ring up-tide. As it sank the tide washed the net and chapstick off the frame, and by the time it was on the ground it had been pulled round through 180 degrees. Getting a dredge 'heel to tide' meant giving it a deft twist as it was thrown. If a dredge was slipped into the water in what seemed the easiest logical way, if often finished up foul.

When enough warp was paid out, the Essex men caught a half-hitch and back-turn round a rough thole pin set in the rail (never a clove-hitch) so that if the dredge caught fast the warp surged and could be thrown off, or at worst the thole pin broke. The inboard end of the warp was buoyed so that a foul dredge could be recovered as the smack sailed back. Any old broken spar end was used for a buoy and as it was usually waterlogged it often ran under in a strong tide, sometimes making it necessary to wait for slack water to recover it. On rough ground dredges sometimes had the warp secured to the scraper end and seized to the ring. If the dredge fouled, the seizing broke and the dredge could be recovered capsized. In most other parts of the country, including Kent, Cornwall and Emsworth, the warps were not hitched on tholes but secured by toggles of light yarn, which broke in emergency. One advantage of this was that, as the tide ebbed, the rolling hitch of the warp could be moved down, ensuring that the right amount of warp was always played out. Even with these precautions dredges were sometimes lost. Ted Pitt recalls losing a set of seven while dredging in Harwich Harbour, when the wash of a packet boat rolled the smack so violently that all the warps parted. How the deep-sea dredges were secured on the big Essex smacks no-one is now left to recall. But cetainly in the Emsworth fleet toggles were always used – six a side on the cutters, eight a side on the ketches and twelve a side on the mighty *Echo*.

With her dredges hove, the smack's sails were if possible adjusted so she lay square to the tide, sweeping the widest possible path. To make her follow the required course, steering was not by the tiller, but by adjusting the peak of the mainsail. Fully peaked up, the sail drove the smack ahead; slacked down, or 'rucked', it made her stop or fall astern. I have spent many a morning working a narrow Essex creek avoiding withies, yacht moorings and other obstructions, continually setting up the peak halyard and then easing it away again. The Brightlingsea smacks, which were used principally in the open estuary, and so did not have to perform the tricks required at Mersea or Paglesham, never rucked their peaks, insisting that the boats were too big and the gear too heavy for this manoeuvre. They preferred to trice up the tack of the mainsail, which shortened sail but did not contribute so much to manoeuvrability. It was common in the Colne to see smacks (and the river police boats imitating them) with the tack triced right up to the gaff jaws – something never seen in the Blackwater or Roach.

*Unloading oysters at
Tollesbury.*

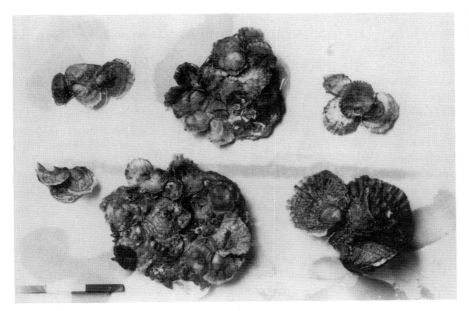

One-year old oyster spat still attached to the shells on which they settled.

Under the favourable conditions I have described a smack would, on reaching the end of her ground, go about on the other tack and sail back over the tide to repeat the operation. Sometimes, however, this was not possible. In calms, or if the wind was too light to sail over the tide, a smack might have to make one drive over her ground and bring up, lying to a dredge if the tide was not too strong, to await more wind or the turn of the tide. If the wind was against the tide, the smack was driven as close to the wind as possible on the more favourable tack, making a slanting board over the ground. This was called 'haul-and-end', and made hard work, for the dredges streamed astern and thus involved heavy heaving.

The deep-heeled smacks which took the prizes at the annual regatta, such as Tom French's *Unity*, perhaps the most perfect of all the small oyster smacks, and certainly one of the most admired, could work their dredges to windward much better than the shallower boats such as the *Betty*, a successful example of the type, or Cassell French's *Mersea Lass*, which was never an easy boat to work. But under more normal conditions, towing to leeward, the shallower draught boats had an advantage, for their lack of grip on the water allowed them to slide over the ground, while the *Unity* stood to her dredges like a pilot cutter. And when the fleet was working on shallow ground, such as 'The Main', they could get in an hour's work after the ebb had driven the deeper boats off into the estuary. With strong tides and a light foul-wind an alternative expedient was 'logging' which involved stowing all sails and allowing the tide to carry the smack broadside. Careful adjustment of the dredges was necessary to keep her in this position and in particular the bow and stern dredges had to be hauled simultaneously. But this dodge was more commonly employed for beam trawling. Using the expedients described the experienced dredgerman could usually find some ground where the conditions of wind and tide enabled him to work.

When the dredge had been down for perhaps five or ten minutes, according to the condition of the ground, the time came to haul. The rough bass warps, full of sharp shell and grit, were hard on the hands, and the dredge was heavy with mud and weed, so the dredgerman was not sorry to see the ring break the surface of the water. He could now lodge the iron 'heel' fixed below the ring on the smack's rail, so it took the weight before he pulled the frame across the rail, to allow the bag hanging overboard to drain, and perhaps 'docking' it in the water once or twice to wash out some of the mud. Worst of all were stones, often picked up under the Colne Bar and up the Blackwater on the 'Stone Grounds' by Thirslet Creek. They were cruelly heavy and there was no way of washing them out of the net.

The dredgerman next grabbed the chapstick, emptied the contents on deck, hove the dredge again and got down to sorting out what it had brought up. Marketable oysters were cleared of barnacles and other growths and went into a tub. Brood and ware were carefully removed from the culch or other material on which they had spatted, using a blunt knife called a cultac, and 'singled' if they were growing in a cluster. The final 'cull' usually awaited the end of the day's work. In the summer the whole catch would go back on the laying, or in the case of the Tollesbury and Mersea boats on a selected fattening patch in Thornfleet, which corresponded to the Colne Company's Pyefleet. In the selling season, the laying-holder would sort oysters, ware and brood into different pits, ready for different markets. Pests, such as slipper limpets, five-fingers and whelk tingles were set aside for destruction ashore, though on common ground

Oyster measures, including a tub (4 wash), half-tub (2 wash), a wash, peck and half-wash.

Mature five-year old oysters.

everything was often recklessly dumped overboard with the exception of a few five-fingers which the dredgermen might like to take home to put on his garden, or if it was the asparagus season a tendil of black seaweed for the same purpose.

All the rest, shell and rubbish, was gathered up by a pair of boards called shards and tossed overboard, with any crabs trying to make an escape crushed underfoot. The Whitstable smacks had scuppers cut in their bulwarks so the rubbish could be pushed overboard without lifting it off the deck, but the Essex men never adopted this labour-saving device, chiefly because they were not prepared to spoil the appearance of their elegant yacht-like craft, and also perhaps because they used them for fish trawling,

Working dredges on the deck of a smack.

and it was not a good idea to provide a place where a nice two-pound sole could wriggle overboard before you could grab him. It was also argued that with shards the rubbish could be broadcast and scattered, whereas when merely pushed through a scupper it all sank in a heap.

The flush-decked Essex smacks made hard work of dredging compared to the half-decked boats preferred at Southampton and in Cornwall, where you could stand up in comfort, hauling the dredge to the side deck and culling out the contents there at table height. As one Cornishman put it, 'I wouldn't want an Essex boat, working all day doubled up with your arse in the air and your head down between your knees with the boom likely to knock you overboard any minute.'[3] But the difference was that on the clean Truro grounds the dredges came up with little more than light loads of shell. In Essex they were heavy with weed and soil, and to get them on deck you needed to brace your boot against the rail and use the strength of your legs.

The smacks were also used on layings in the creeks, though to a less extent at Mersea than at Tollesbury, where some grounds became almost unworkable because of the spoil culch dumped by smacks halfway down them. After the smack had turned at the end of her haul, emptying dredges on deck, the rubbish was cast overboard on the sail back, so that the layings developed deep water at each end with a hill in the middle.

The fishermen's boats known as bumkins could also work a single dredge under favourable conditions, which however, were not common. These were heavy clinker-built gaff-rigged sloops, with short iron bowsprits giving them their name, usually built with sawn frames. They were not the same as the smaller 'winkle brigs' which were usually built with steamed frames, and lugsail rigged, though in recent years the distinction has been lost and boats of both classes are described by either name.

At Mersea the chief method of creek cultivation was known as 'haul-tow'. It was a back-breaking business and required skill to lay the anchors in the best position to suit wind and tide. For the first few traverses the skiff could be sheered across a little for each haul; then the anchors had to be moved to cover the next strip. The method was much favoured by Peter French's cousin Leslie for his laying in Salcott Creek. Peter recalls that as a boy he was asked to work there but his father thought this no way to break a fourteen-year-old boy's back and suggested using his motor boat to tow the skiff. The idea was heresy to Leslie. 'Haul-tow', he explained earnestly 'is the essence of dredging.'[4]

Haul-tow became obsolete in Essex before World War II with the introduction of motor skiffs, which were modelled on the bumkins and the transom-sterned boats used for transporting sprats rather than on the double-ended oyster boats. Powered by slow-running 'Brit' petrol engines (the only internal combustion engine to retain the intrinsic charm of the steam engines they vaguely resembled), the motor skiffs took over the task of cultivating the creek layings for their last twenty years, and were still being built in the 1950s.

The smacks remained faithful to sail – the last Essex fishing boats to do so – partly because there was never a lot of money to spare in the oyster trade, and in particular there was no prospect of the sort of bonanza catch which sometimes provided other fishermen with capital or tempted them into borrowing in the hopes one would turn up; partly because sailing craft could still meet the needs of dredging, and in fact did it better than motor boats, which towed their dredges in a straight and narrow line, catching less stock and doing more damage to the ground than the smacks which swept a wide path, sheering about and generally harrowing the ground as they did so. The dredgermen on the Truro grounds were so convinced that motorised craft would destroy them that they resolved as long ago as the First World War never to permit dredging under power, and have remained faithful to that policy to the present day. Haul-tow has also survived there – under the name tow-haul – using an ingenious little double windlass never introduced in Essex. The skiff is anchored, and some thirty to fifty fathoms of warp paid out as it is rowed over the ground to be dredged. The dredge is then put out on a length of warp appropriate to the depth of water. The skiff is now hauled back, using one drum of the windlass, and the dredge pulled up using the other.

The oysterman's year

The oysterman's own patch was his special pride and joy, as well as his frequent worry and anxiety, but in the age of traditional native oyster cultivation he spent most of his time dredging 'outside'. Only in the later age of the 'Ports' trade did men spend all their working hours on their own allotments.

This account of the traditional oysterman's working year is based on Mersea. It is probably broadly representative of other Essex centres with many local variations which are now difficult to discover, for only at Mersea did the old ways go on up to World War II, with half-a-dozen smacks still employed exclusively on oystering and doing no other work the whole of their long lives.

The annual cycle began in the New Year, as the oysterman set to work to clean his grounds. The winter's accumulation of mud had to be cleared off the edges of the laying, using a 'slud driver' – a piece of wood fixed to a handle with which the mud was pushed off into the channel. Then the surface had to be made up flat, hard and level with 'shram', and sometimes with chalk and stone. The creek bed itself also required a clean-up, using a harrow, which in sailing days was a dredge frame with no rigging, but with the scythe replaced by a bar through which were driven three-inch iron pegs about nine inches apart, though with the introduction of power craft iron land harrows came into use. Again the object was to achieve as firm and flat a bed as possible, clearing the soft mud away and reducing the hills and holes, for oysters falling in hollows were liable to be 'slobbed over' with mud. Dredging tended to deepen holes and raise ridges and to counter this a couple of harrows were sometimes towed along with working dredges, being lifted only when the end of the ground was reached. In the deeper creeks, such as Tollesbury and Salcott the bottom was never seen by the owner; elsewhere it was revealed on spring ebbs. Peter remembers his father looking forward to such an opportunity for an overdue inspection of his ground in the Strood Channel, only to remark when he saw it that he wished it had remained under water, for it was in a much less perfect state than he had hoped.

Before he stepped out of his boat on to his edge, the oysterman always put on a pair of splashers – boards with rope loops to slip over his boots – for a few footprints soon ruined level ground. Splashers were also used in pits, which required similar attention. These played an important part in the work of all cultivators, with the exception of a very few small operators, owning perhaps an eighty-yard stretch of 'Doitch', who were content to lay their produce on their edges and sell out completely at the season's end.

Most small growers needed at least a couple of pits; the more substantial ones up to a dozen. While the Tollesbury and Mersea Co. pits on Packing Marsh were laid out in a neat line, most pits were dug haphazard in any convenient bit of level saltings. They were submerged at spring tides, so that for most of the time they were undisturbed, but every fortnight got a topping up and some change of water. They were about three feet deep, so that when they were full the oysterman worked about knee-deep in the water. Their bottoms were floored with 'shram', and sometimes, though not often, their walls were boarded. Concrete was occasionally used, as at the notorious condemned pits by the Hard at Brightlingsea, but out on the remote saltings it was impracticable, and in any case was considered liable to conduct frost.

Pits were of any convenient size, and would be known as 'fifty-wash pits' or 'hundred-wash pits'. Countless hours of back-breaking toil must have gone into spitting out the heavy clay; up to fifty years ago there was at least one professional pit-digger at Mersea, reckoning to take a fortnight to construct an average-size pit. The weakest point was the dam, necessary to empty the pit for cleaning and maintenance. Within living memory most pits were dammed merely by blocking the outlet channel with mud, leaving a place too low and weak for safety. It then became the custom to fit a wooden shutter, set in an angle-iron frame, which could be raised like a mill or lock sluice. This often had a hole in the centre, covered by a hinged wooden flap on the inside, so that it could be pushed open for a rising tide to replenish the pit, but was held shut by the water pressure as the tide ebbed. This arrangement required wooden wedges and bits of sacking to keep it as nearly watertight as possible, and ultimately it was found better to use a length of sewer pipe, with a bundle of sacks or a wooden plug driven in each end. Apart from wind and weather, crabs were liable to burrow out holes through which a pit could leak away, specially near the dams, for which reason in winter time the oysterman needed to visit his pits daily. While a full pit could withstand all but the worst winters, oysters on the bottom of an empty pit would be killed by a few degrees of frost. The ubiquitous crabs, which easily crushed and ate brood, were also capable of devouring a weakened fully-grown oyster, but this had its advantages for in such a condition it was probably near death anyway, and liable to contaminate its healthy neighbours. The winkle, on the other hand, was an indispensable ally, grazing off weed and keeping pits clean, for which reason a bushel or two were always thrown in.

The sluice pipes, known as 'hooves', were formerly made of long sections of elm, each scooped out on one side and clamped together to form a tube about nine inches in diameter, or, in the case of the Tollesbury and Mersea Co. pits on Mersea Packing Marsh, were square, made of four planks. Later, iron or concrete pipes came to be used.

Some of the more sophisticated sets of pits were provided with a reservoir or backwater to hold a reserve water supply. This made it safer to drain a pit to collect stock from it, without leaving it dry till the next high water.

If, say, less than half the contents were required, they would be taken out without emptying the pit. This could be done using a net on a long handle called a 'didal', or more usually at Mersea by a close-tined fork called an 'evil' or 'heavel'.

Some small pits were known as 'ledgens', perhaps because they were temporary lodging places for oysters. In 1883 the Tollesbury and Mersea Co. decided to put an order for sixteen bushels 'in the ledgen', and when the Mersea 'jury' protested at stock being left out over the winter it was agreed to lay on ten smacks to get the ware into 'ledgens' and the half-ware into the pits. Alternatively it is possible these 'ledgens' were floating wooden tanks. An example, with a little 'office' or store built at one end, survived opposite Stone Hill House at West Mersea into the 1940s, and was called 'The Legend'. The 'floating boxes' condemned at Southend in the 1890s may have been something of this sort, for though I have never heard of anything like the Mersea 'legend' I do not suppose it was unique. The Tollesbury and Mersea Co. records are, however, so detailed that such a construction would probably have been recorded.

The dredge also had to be kept busy on the layings, partly because its action harrowed away mud, partly to show the cultivator the state of his stock, and partly to clear away pests. The worst of these were whelk tingles, which could bore into a young oyster, 'five-fingers' (starfish), which could clasp an oyster till it opened, and in later years slipper limpets. Mussels also cluttered up oyster grounds; for some reason, while in Norfolk they were considered more valuable for cultivation than oysters, in Essex they were only dredged as a fertiliser for farmers' fields. The Colne Company permitted its members to take them, but when this did not keep them down in 1892 the Board paid 4 shillings a bushel for their removal, 'relying on farmers' tallies'. 'Ross', a sandy coraline growth made by small red worms on which pink shrimps thrived, was a nuisance, especially in Colne, where 'the Ross Hill' was condemned in 1892 and 'the rosy ground' was referred to in 1913. Blubber weed, also known as sea squirts or vulgarly 'pissers', flourished in the same conditions which suited oyster growth, for which reason its first appearance was welcomed, but thereafter it had to be cleared away. The *Pyefleet II* was taken out of retirement in 1934 to harrow it in the Colne. Sea urchins were blamed for scraping spat off culch, and yet other ailments were 'pock', a small red growth which badly affected the Blackwater in 1846,[1] and a white cement-like deposit which made scrawly patterns on the shells, giving it the name 'German writing'.

'Greening' was a phenomenon which paradoxically did no harm to oysters, but caused more damage to fisheries than some of the pests mentioned. Equally paradoxically, it was formerly a mark of excellence; latterly a market disqualification.

In the seventeenth century it was said of oysters that 'the best in England, fat, green-finned, are bred near Colchester where they have an excellent art to feed them in pits for that purpose'.[2] The Brightlingsea droitgatherer of the Cinque Ports in 1620 was sending the Lord Warden a weekly consignment of 'two firkins of oshters by the Colchester carriers, one greene and the other greate oshters'.[3]

The green tinge was caused by a diatom found in shallow water. It appeared in the 'beard', sometimes called the 'gills' or 'fins'; that is, the tissue surrounding the plump meat, and it could not be seen till the oyster was opened. This meant it could only be detected by wasting time and oysters on opening samples, or the yet more wasteful alternative of waiting for a consignment to be rejected. Some of the Brightlingsea pits greened oysters, but they were not used for this purpose after 1825, by which time white oysters came to be preferred in the English market, probably as consumers became more purity-conscious as the result of poisoning 'scares', for the discoloration resembled another less pleasant form of greening caused by copper in Welsh and Cornish waters.

By the end of the century greening was spoiling the market for Blackwater oysters, which had to be sent to Whitstable, where a few months on the flats removed the colour, and in the Colne, the Pyefleet fattening ground was not extended higher up the creek because of a fear of greening there. Yet green oysters remained in favour in Paris, probably because the French were used to those grown in *parcs*, or *claires* as they were called at Marennes – big shallow lagoons which covered only at spring tides and so became brackish. In 1884 George Harvey & Son of Wivenhoe, whose layings in Tollesbury Creek are described in a later chapter, issued a leaflet advertising 'the green-finned native', which had been popular on the continent for a century as *'les huitres verts d'Ostend'*. Testimonials to their purity included the curious claim by Dr. Frank Buckland, the naturalist and Inspector of Fisheries, that 'this vegetable pigment imparts a peculiar taste and agreeable flavour to the meat of these plump little oysters'.[4]

The 'shram' used for making up both edges and pit bottoms was broken shell deposited by the natural action of the tides in a great heap on the now vanished Nass spit, about halfway between the Nass beacon and the end of the Tollesbury saltings. Not only did nature provide this convenient supply, it also graded it, with the finest stuff (used for chicken grit, even after the opening of the shell crushing plant during the First World War) at the east end, and the largest shell, suitable for culch, at the west end. On a suitable calm day the skiff would be laid alongside the 'shram' hill and deep-loaded from the central part of the hill for the purposes mentioned. The chance might also be taken to bring up a load of culch from the western end to be stored close to the laying for use later in the summer. Before the introduction of motor skiffs a sailing bumkin came in handy for this work.

Having completed his spring cleaning, which in practice only involved a few days' or weeks' work, the oysterman settled down by mid-March to his daily routine of dredging 'outside', that is in the estuary, up to Thirslet before the enclosure by the Tollesbury and Mersea Co., but only below 'the Metes' thereafter, around Colne Bar, down the Wallet, in the Rays'n and Shore Ends, on the Buxey and St. Peter's Flats. Unlike the Maldoners, few Mersea smacks went further afield or spent nights away from home.

27

First one place, then another, proved productive, showing that nature could in some mysterious way achieve haphazard results without any of the careful tending the cultivators needed. Small spat was left on the shell or stone where it had alighted, and was brought home as 'spat shell'; half-ware and larger were carefully parted off, or 'singled' if in a cluster, using a blunt wooden-handled knife known as a cultac. Everything was taken, for perhaps uniquely the Blackwater was the one great fishery which never introduced either a close season or a 'ring' as a measure of the minimum size it was permitted to take.

As soon as a smack found a useful patch she would soon be joined by others, for the prevailing wind usually sent all the smacks to the same ground, and if one of them returned to the same spot several times she was sure to be followed. During World War II the old concrete hulk *Molliette* was sunk on the end of Cocum Bar, just outside the limits of the Colne fishery, for use as a target by American fighter-bombers, which peppered her with thousands of rounds from their guns, resulting in a hail of brass cartridge cases pouring into the water. Getting a dredge full of these, Peter French recognised the possibilities, and began to work the patch in earnest. Before long there were half a dozen other smacks around him, indignantly complaining, 'What do you think you're supposed to be up to? Ain't nothing here but a load of old rubbishy shell cases'. To keep the secret, Peter took nothing ashore, but stowed his catch day after day aboard the *Mersea Lass*, till finally the U.S. Air Force inconsiderately fitted catch nets to their planes, and the shower of metal manna ceased to descend from heaven. He then had a highly satisfactory settle-up with Wheeler and the Manganese Bronze and Brass Co.

The smacks working the common grounds were all competing against each other, yet by some custom or tradition, as soon as one decided the day's work was done, all sailed home together, even if one or two lingered for a final haul. Back on their grounds they laid the day's catch in the middle of the creek or on the edges according to the nature of their grounds. In Salcott most went on to the clean creek bed; in Strood and 'doitch' some were put on the edges and some in the creeks. Only the Tollesbury north channel layings – 'the finest oyster ground in the world', as Tom French, skipper of the *Unity*, liked to proclaim them – made little use of edges till they came to be employed for laying 'Ports'.

As spring turned to summer, thoughts turned to the prospect of spatfall. The oysters gave the first sign by turning 'white sick' and then, just before spawning, 'black sick'. For a successful spatfall the water temperature had to exceed sixty degrees Fahrenheit, and by early June thermometers were busily employed seeking this condition. Culching was redoubled, for the shell was considered to be at its best after a fortnight in the water. As the newly released spat fell, shell was constantly examined for the first tiny white spots. 'Clocks' (old empty unparted shells) were split open and laid on the rail to dry. The old hands took the spectacles off their noses and produced magnifying glasses from their waistcoat pockets to examine them. It took a sharp eye and long experience to be sure that the little pinpoints were the first sign of oysters, and not barnacles or limpets. Soon, however, there was no other topic of conversation. At worst no spat appeared as summer wore on – a disaster. Two spat on a shell was better than nothing, but not much good. Ten or twelve on a shell meant the prospect of a brood bounty next year. A report in 1876 claimed that up to 80 spat had been found on shells in the Crouch and Roach – an astonishing figure even for a notably prolific area.

By Mersea tradition the earliest date spat was ever seen was 12 June. No-one knew what year this occurred, or who detected it, but the date was firmly fixed in folklore.

Efforts to clean edges and layings were redoubled, using dredge and harrow. Then the culching started, spreading loads of clean shell from the eastern end of the Nass 'shram' hill, and sometimes from a heap of 'blue' shell on Thirslet Spit. Most precious of all was the 'blue' culch from the Nore sand, dredged largely by Tollesbury smacks which sold it to the Colne and T. & M. companies at a shilling a tub. The exact nature and cause of 'blue' culch is obscure; probably it was very old shell which had been buried under London clay. The fact that the Nore produced such vast supplies suggests that this sand must once have been a great oyster ground – further striking evidence of the ubiquitous profusion of oysters in ancient days.

Culch dredging was a full-time winter occupation for some Tollesbury smacks, which brought hundreds of tons from The Cant (the flats off the Kentish shore) into the Crouch, laying it on the saltings opposite the Pile House below Burnham till it was needed in June. The demand for culch in the Crouch and Roach was immense, due to the great areas under cultivation and the quality of the husbandry, leading to a fracas described in Chapter 13. Nature provided these rivers with a 'shram' hill on the Foulness Ridge sand, bigger than the one at Mersea, and in addition to this Prior's sailing barge *Jesse* also made regular voyages to Leigh to bring freights of broken cockle shell.

The middles and edges now required to be left alone for the spat to settle and take hold, and the oystermen resumed their routine of dredging 'outside' for a few more months, varying this with an occasional week's work for 'the Company', when their turn came round, till (in living memory) the date of the Whitstable boats' first visit was announced. The marketing in earlier days is not clearly recorded, though there are still memories of French fishing boats loading freight and of their crews making merry in the old Victory Inn. Doubtless merchants such as Sanford of Wivenhoe played a role, though Mersea itself seems to have developed no major dealers. By the mid-nineteenth century, however, Mersea was working almost entirely for Whitstable, and the arrival of the Kentish carriers was in later years the high point of the year, if only because it brought the prospect of some much needed payments.

The Whitstable Co. sent the *Postboy*, and the Seasalter and Ham Co. the *Seasalter*, which could stow a thousand wash in her hold. The Tollesbury AEFA (formerly *Emma Jane*) joined in the carrying, with the three smacks freighting oysters and brood as fast as they could make the journeys up to the 1920s. Thereafter the visits decreased to two or three a year, made by the Whitstable Company's *Thomas Foord*, a full-bellied old carrier, and the Seasalter and Ham Company's beautiful clipper-bowed ketch *Speedwell*, which took over after the *Seasalter* was broken up in the late 1930s. [5]

Against the coming of the carriers, stocks began to be gathered into the pits, and when they arrived the smacks swarmed around them. The bags were emptied into the Kentish men's half-tub measures as gently as possible to maintain the bulk of their content, with the Kentish men giving the tubs a kick to make the oysters settle. The Mersea men, never adventurous or enterprising over marketing, accepted their role as suppliers to rival fisheries as a long-standing fact of life, though there was plenty of grumbling over the way the two companies fixed the prices between them.

The dredging season thus ended by mid-September. With most of the saleable oysters gone, the next task was to get the half-ware and brood into the pits against the winter. The most accessible pits were used for the larger stuff, wanted for sale; the more remote pits for brood which would not be needed till next year. Laying oysters was a skilled job, always undertaken by the master, who allowed his assistant only to hand him the tendils. The oysters had to be closely spaced to use the pit effectively, but they must not touch for if one died it would infect anything in contact with it. One of the dreaded sights was a round black patch of dead stock, spreading outwards from the original source of the sickness, recalling the 'ring o'roses' which in the nursery rhyme is said to recall the spread of plague spots. It did not matter which way up they lay, though their natural centre of gravity caused most to fall flat side up.

Such was the oysterman's year. What of the days that made up that year? The oysterman turned out at six a.m. to be at work by seven, and knocked off at two, to be home about three. This working day long preceded the T. & M. Co. but was incorporated in its rules and practices. But before he had an engine to help him he did not want to face a whole ebb tide in order to reach his mooring. Thus the ritual of the 'short tides' was observed. Starting on the first day before the full moon, the working day ended at high water (around noon), and so continued for a few days till the normal three p.m. knock-off time was restored. To compensate, the oystermen would often, on five o'clock tides, work on till four in summer or dark in winter. Many Mersea men took advantage of this early day to turn in as soon as they had got home and had something to eat. After an hour or two in bed, they would get up, shave, put on shore clothes and be ready to face the world. Cassell French assured me that making two days out of every one

Raking level the edge of a bed after collecting oysters for market. Note the 'splashers' on the feet to keep the surface flat.

got the best out of life. But though Peter was drawn towards many of the old traditions, and for a while tried this one, he soon found it did not suit his restless spirit.

The technique with foreign re-laid oysters such as 'Ports' was altogether different. There was, of course, no 'outside' dredging, so the smack was not needed. In the 1930s however, sailing bumkins were hard worked, carrying loads to and from the grounds and dredging in the creeks. After the Second World War the creek beds were less used, with a concentration on edges, some of which were extended above low water mark for the purpose. With this sort of cultivation, most of the work was done at low water, walking the grounds in splashers to cull and collect stock for market and to clean the grounds of pests. Some cultivators preferred to use a dredge at high water, claiming that the ground could be swept more efficiently in this way, with the oysters sorted according to size as they were returned to different areas. But most considered that to obtain the rapid growth which was all-important, the 'Ports' should not be disturbed or damaged by the dredge, and patiently worked by hand over every square yard of their edges at least once a fortnight, with more frequent visits when the stock for sale in the pits required to be replenished. With this method, which was less dependent on tides and weather conditions, a dredge was used only at neap tides, when for a few days each fortnight the edges did not come a-dry. The seed oysters were, however, always laid from a skiff, as in this way they could be scattered more evenly. The lorries arriving from the London docks were persuaded to back down the Hard into the water so the skiffs could come alongside and load the wicker baskets. As each basket was emptied it was tossed overboard, leaving hundreds bobbing about in the creeks to be eagerly picked up as they blew ashore by those glad of a handsome free container for logs or apples.

Considering that they were foreigners from southern climates, 'Ports' were surprisingly hardy – so much so that the leading Mersea grower did not even put them in pits for the winter, preferring to leave them undisturbed on their edges, which were carefully tended and strewn with winkles to graze off weed. Foreign and native oyster cultivation were thus two different trades, not easily mixed though, in a clean-bottomed creek like Salcott or Tollesbury, 'Ports' could be kept on the edges, with natives laid off in the channel. The two trades however, complemented each other, since 'Ports' were sold in summer, 'till the lights were turned off at Blackpool'. Indeed after the mortalities and failing spatfalls of the 1920s, the traditional native culture could only be sustained with some supplementary support.

CHAPTER THREE

How Colchester claimed the Colne

The three great Essex oyster estuaries each had its own special character. The Colne was controlled with a fierce possessive pride by Colchester Corporation; the Blackwater was common ground, open to all, with extensive private layings in the creeks of West Mersea, Tollesbury and Salcott; while the Crouch was the property of the lords of the Manor of Burnham, though the Roach was common ground, with the exception of private layings within it.

Colchester's rights over the Colne date back to a charter granted to the town in 1189 by Richard I, with a reference to 'the time of Henry his grandfather', which takes them back to at least 1100. Dredging licences were granted for over five centuries at Admiralty courts, when trespassers and other offenders were prosecuted before a jury. These licences were granted not only to Colchester townsmen, but to residents of St. Osyth, Brightlingsea, Alresford, West Mersea, East Mersea, Langenhoe, Fingringhoe and East Donyland (Rowhedge).

In 1683 the Corporation began to lease the fishery, first, till the end of the century, to William Garland and Anthony Sewell, described as mariners of East Mersea, then for twenty-three years to John Potter and Ralph Crefield, who were Colchester 'woollen drapers and aldermen'. They in turn issued licences to dredgermen. This regime may have seen the start of latter-day oyster farming, for it was observed in 1702 that the scientific cultivation of the oyster was 'confined to some few narrow creeks of one single county'.[1] This reference is probably to the Colne.

When in 1740 Colchester's Borough Charter was suspended, the town was left without Mayor, Aldermen or Justices capable of holding Admiralty courts or controlling the fishery, which for some years was freely pillaged. To end this the Colne Fishery Act of 1758 restored the old powers to the Justices of the Peace till the charter was restored in 1763.

Colchester Corporation's claim to the Colne has not gone undisputed. The hereditary Freemen of the town long maintained a belief that the fishery belonged to them, not to the Corporation, and made unsuccessful legal attempts to establish their claim in 1856 and 1898.[2] The Corporation also had to fight off a grant of the fishery in 1447 by Henry VI to his favourite, the Earl of Oxford.

But the chief challenges were from the riverside manors, starting in 1362 with the Lord of the Manor of Langenhoe, Lionel de Bradenham. Sir Roger

Townsend, Lord of the Manor of Wivenhoe, in 1629 contended that 'West Ness', the limit of the fishery prescribed in the charter, was near Wivenhoe, and that he was thus empowered to fish in the part of the river abutting his manor below this point, but the decision was in favour of the town. A later lord of the Manor of Langenhoe (Earl Waldegrave) claimed in 1724 that creeks including Pyefleet and Peewit Island belonged to his manor, but the action was not proceeded with.

Lionel de Bradenham's case was the most important, for he claimed ancient rights enjoyed by the men of Colchester, Alresford, Brightlingsea, St. Osyth, East and West Mersea, Fingringhoe, Peldon, Little Wigborough, Salcott, Tollesbury and Goldhanger. As the historian of Brightlingsea, Dr. E. P. Dickin observes, 'It will be noted that Colchester is in the same boat with the other towns. Her rights are no better than theirs, and there is no hint of the Colne being her exclusive fishery. It was common to them all. It is not likely that, if she had then an exclusive right to the fishery, the fact would not have been mentioned. Richard I's charter (1189) to Colchester confirming her right to the fishery does not even hint that it was exclusively hers. It was inevitable that in time Colchester should get it exclusively. A large and wealthy Corporation, with its prescriptive rights confirmed by Royal Charter, had an enormous advantage over the unorganised fishermen, good as their prescriptive right was. The inevitable came in 1462 when Edward IV granted to the Corporation exclusive rights in the river.'

This view is supported by the fact that Colchester never claimed rights in Brightlingsea Creek, even though the charter specified 'all places called the creeks in the same water'. Dickin even speculates that Colchester cheated by shifting the goal posts, and claiming that the much-disputed West Ness was Colne Point, well below Brightlingsea, though a local tradition insists that it referred to West Marsh Point, immediately above the creek. Two Colchester mariners in 1630 deposed that it was six miles from Colchester and four from Wivenhoe, which would certainly support West Marsh Point.[3]

There were two further manorial challenges at the end of the nineteenth century. The Gazelet shore, below Brightlingsea Creek, was improved for cultivation in 1883, including the making of a bank 10 yards wide. Trespassing here, probably at the instigation of the lord of the Manor of St. Osyth, caused the Corporation to bring an action in 1897, when the Queen's Bench confirmed the manorial rights to the soil. An appeal failed to upset this judgment, but gave the Corporation the right to work the ground as they had since 1883.[4]

The second challenge, by the Manor of Brightlingsea, for Alresford Creek, was a spirited affair. It started with the laying of oysters there, by Corporation licence in 1899, but the Board then decided against further leases. In 1902, however, a barge arrived with 200 baskets of Portuguese (or 'Spanish') oysters which were laid by Horace Day of Brightlingsea who had been concerned in the previous venture and who claimed to have sold a *How Colchester* thousand bushels to William Ormes, of Bishopsgate Street, who had *claimed the Colne* leased the Creek from Benjamin Colet. The *Pyefleet* dredged them up, also removing some withies, whereupon Pulleyne, Lord of the Manor of Brightlingsea, alleging them to have been stolen, issued a writ. At the same time another barge-load arrived, with Pulleyne refusing to pay tonnage dues on the grounds that they had been unloaded within his manor. The *Pyefleet* again dredged these up and after Pulleyne had refused to accept them, re-laid them in the river.

The case was heard in 1904 before the Lord Chief Justice, who found for the Corporation, with a similar result on appeal, though the Corporation then failed to establish its claim to ownership of the bed of the creek and foreshore and was awarded less than total costs.[5]

Perhaps prompted by a desire to avoid another such legal imbroglio, the Corporation in 1901 bought the layings in the North and South Geedons Creeks, along with Rat Island, for £2,300.

The Geedons layings were originally part of the Manor of Fingringhoe, a Colneside village which features in medieval fishing history, but thereafter seems to have turned its back on the water and showed no interest in oystering. In the eighteenth century the grounds were let to Sanford of Wivenhoe, but when his lease expired in 1800 he refused to renew it at £70 a year. Since no other lessee could be found he secured a new seven-year tenancy at £50, but he was paying £75 when the Manor was sold up in 1809, and again when the layings were sold as part of Wick Farm in 1812.[6] In 1867 five layings in these creeks were leased by W Heath of Wivenhoe from Sir Richard Affleck at £30 a year, and by 1890 they were in the occupation of Harvey and his ill-fated Colchester Native Oyster Fishery Company. But at the time of their sale to the Corporation, they belonged to W. Stammers of Brightlingsea. They were not incorporated into the Colne Fishery till 1943, but were let by the Corporation to James Heath till 1917, and thereafter to Superintendent Poole of the River Police, who is remembered to have tried laying clams there.

As a result of these disputes and decisions, Brightlingsea Creek was thus left as the only independent fishery in the Colne. It was probably common ground till around 1660 when pits and layings begin to be mentioned. Brightlingsea being a 'limb' of the Cinque Ports, the Lord Warden appointed a 'droit gatherer' to preserve his rights, especially over his own layings. These included taking young oysters in any part of the Colne (evidence that even when Colchester's monopoly had been established by the later charter of 1462 Brightlingsea still refused to acknowledge it) and the appointment of the 'summer dredger'.

The summer dredger was an ancient office, recurrent throughout many fisheries. It represents a common feature among customs and practices which were generally diverse and individual, prompting curiosity as to its origin and underlining the importance of a trade which was relied on as a regular provider of charitable relief. In 1579 the Bailiff of Brightlingsea notified the Bailiffs of Colchester that 'according to our custome at auncient usage we have appointed . . . Thomas Fortune and Thomas Arnolde to be oure Sommer Dreiger for this yere, the one for the service of . . . the Lord of our mannor, and the other for oure Towne. And for that they are very poore men we have placed them both in one boate'.[7]

Colchester Corporation, according to Morant, had been accustomed since Elizabethan times to grant a free licence for 'a summer's dredging' to one poor man for each of the eight Colneside parishes.[8]

The regulations of the Ipswich fishery, described in Chapter 9, in 1578 provided that 'the Bayliffs . . . may licence any impotent or lame person to dredge oysters in the Haven at pleasure provided that there be but one person in the bote and that none but well grown oysters be carried away'.[9]

An acute shortage of oysters in the 1630s led in 1638 to a national ban on all exports (with exceptions in favour of the Prince of Orange and the

A map of oyster-pits in the saltings and foreshore at Brightlingsea, emphasising the extent of the trade a century ago.

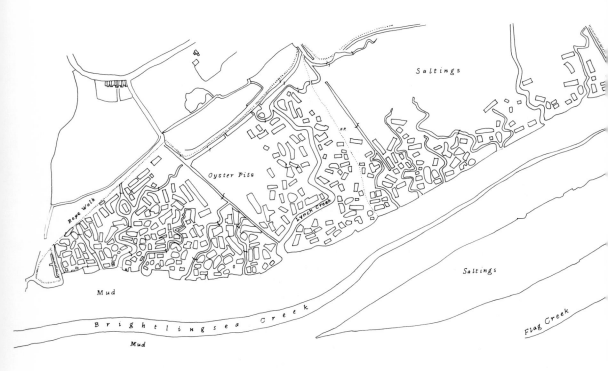

Queen of Bohemia, who was the daughter of King James) and other restrictions including an order to the Corporation of Colchester to cease licensing persons to dredge in the close season.

By 1675 the office may have lost its charitable character, for in that year an East Donyland fisherman paid five shillings to the Manor of Walton for a year's licence 'to be summer dredger to dredge and take oysters in the river or water called Hantford Waters . . . (sizeable ware) with a smack or boate, himself and another man in the boate with him, according to the custome in that behalfe used'.[10]

The creekside layings developed and proliferated till in 1848 White's *Gazetteer and Directory of Essex* listed 27 oyster merchants and smack owners at Brightlingsea – the only place to be credited with this trade classification. With some sixty smacks working between Jersey and Spurn Head on deep-sea dredging, the stay-at-homes providing the majority of the Colne Fishery's licence holders, and the later company establishing its headquarters in the town, Brightlingsea became one of the great centres of the trade in its final heyday, as is more fully described in Chapter 10.

Even more important in the eighteenth century was Wivenhoe, noted by Defoe in 1724 as, 'where they (oysters) are laid in beds or pits on the shoar to feed, as they call it; and then, being barrelled up and carried to Colchester (which is but three miles off), they are sent to London by land, and are, from thence, called Colchester oysters'.[11] Colchester itself was too far up its tidal river to play any active part in its fishery, and the Corporation was content to milk the profits (though less ready to underwrite losses or capital expenditure) and to enjoy some civic beanfeasts, of which the best known were the ancient annual opening ceremony, with the bewigged Town Clerk reading the Charter on a smack's deck in Pyefleet, and the company regaling themselves on gin and gingerbread, and the less historical Oyster Feast in the Town Hall, both carried on to this day. There was formerly also an annual civic ceremony of closing or 'setting' the fishery at the season's end.

Hence the importance of Wivenhoe, where an early nineteenth century journal kept by William Sanford, a merchant who lived on the quay in Trinity House, gives a vivid picture of the trade which by the end of the eighteenth century was far from the mere cultivation of one's patch and the disposal of its harvest.[12]

Sanford and his brother had their own layings at Tollesbury, where between 1810 and 1828 they 'haled' 9,022 wash of marketable oysters, twice the quantity of brood oysters laid. In 1827 they spent £52.10s. on dredging, with rent, taxes, poor rate, stock laid and sundries amounting to £79.12s. – a total expenditure of £317.3s. But they 'haled' 958 wash of marketable oysters worth say, 9 shillings a wash. Between 1816 and 1827 they cleared £1,450, the average yearly profit being £130.

They bought brood from Colne smacks dredging off Norfolk and further north and sailed their marketable oysters to London in Colne smacks, a *continued on opposite page*

A map from early this century of Brightlingsea oyster layings and their holders, most of them old Brightlingsea families.

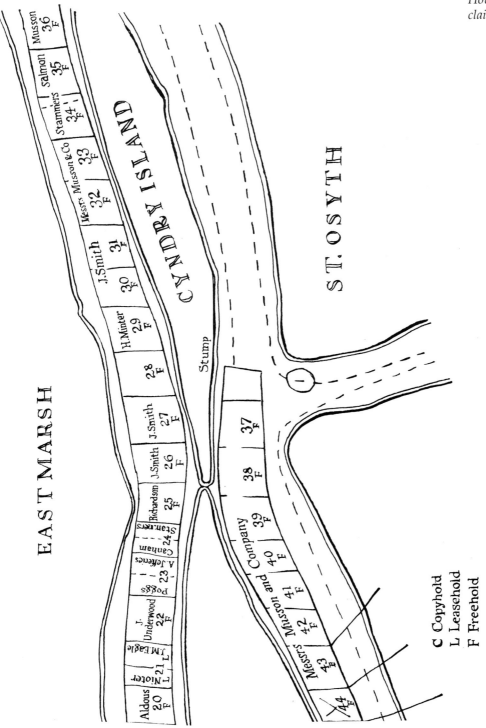

EAST MARSH

CYNDRY ISLAND

ST. OSYTH

Aldous 20 F
T. Nioter 21 L
J.M.Eagle
J. Underwood 22 F
Pogse
A. Jefferies 23
Canham
Stanmers 24
Richardson 25 F
J. Smith 26 F
J. Smith 27 F
28 F
H. Minter 29 F
30 F
J. Smith 31 F
Messrs Musson & Co 32 F
33 F
Stammers 34 F
salmon 35 F
Musson 36 F

37 F
38 F
39 F
40 F
Messrs Musson and Company 41 F
42 F
43 F
44 F

Stump

C Copyhold
L Leasehold
F Freehold

39

service so regular that they are referred to as 'Monday's, Tuesday's and Friday's boats'. Most of the London trade was to fishmongers, but distinguished customers included Lord Howe, First Lord of the Admiralty. Others were sent by 'land conveyance', Sanford's standing orders for 1803 including 'every Tuesday one barrel to the Marquis of Salisbury, at W. Sparrow's, near Ipswich; Thursday two barrels to the Earl of Waldegrave to be left at Mr. Checkers, Chelmsford; Saturday one barrel to the Marquis of Salisbury and a double barrel to the Countess of Waldegrave, to be left at the Lion and Lamb, Brentwood, until called for. Likewise Thursday one barrel to the Hon. William Fitzroy to be left at the King's Head, Norwich'.

Rowhedge also depended on the trade, with 250 dredgermen in 1867, according to J. Willett, a prominent merchant.

Maldon and the Blackwater

Maldon Corporation enjoyed rights over the Blackwater – or 'Pont' as it was known from medieval to recent times, from the river's old name, Panta – conferred by a charter of Henry II in the twelfth century, but on an even more lavish scale than Colchester, for the jurisdiction extended down to the Knoll, a sandbank below Colne Point, and along the coast to Leigh, or as it was recited at the Admiralty Courts:

'From the Stone Bridge to the Hythe, called Maldon Hythe, eastward toward Bradwell to Buherne or Burrow Hills, and from thence to Cratenhay, and so to Rebanke or Kelmspit, which extends to the Creek that parts Ramsgate Stone and Standgate, where formerly hath been a Buoy and since instead thereof hath been set up a Beacon or Sea Mark, and onwards so as to include the whole of the Pont and Blackwater River or Bay, and the Creeks thereof down to the Knowl Sand and from the Knowl Sand to the Buoy on the east end of the Gunfleet and from thence to the Horns Beacon and from thence to the Blacktail Beacon and from thence to Leigh, with the waters and shoals within the said limits.'

The sea marks referred to, from the Knoll to Leigh, were all familiar within living memory, though the reference to the east end of the Gunfleet, beyond Walton Naze, is so extraordinary as to suggest some confusion. The Buherne or Burrow Hills are today known as the Barrow Hills, near the present Mill Beach, while 'Rebank' (formerly Elincroft in the charter of Henry II) is later described as 'about seven miles distant from Maldon', and in a lease of 1756 as 'opposite to a creek called The Wade adjoining to Stansgate'. Cratenhay is nowhere explained. The existence of a creek between what we today call Ramsey Wick and Stansgate is also a reminder that not only its nomenclature has changed, but the estuary itself, through in-walling and tidal erosion. One wonders if those who obtained fishing licences up to the mid-nineteenth century had any idea of the meaning of the words printed on them, or regarded tham as just some archaic litany.

However that may be, for oyster cultivation the Corporation's only active interest was in the upper part of the estuary, 'from Rebank to the garfish weir' – a variation between nominal rights and practical politics which was to cause confusion for seven centuries.

From earliest times Maldon issued licences for at least parts of the fishery, both for dredging oysters and 'muscles' and for 'floating fish', with eels constantly mentioned. The leases from 1587 to 1731 provide a complete list of the tenants and their terms, including in 1705 a provision that 'the said bailiffs [of Maldon] may dredge oysters for their own diet within their own houses', and a repeated exclusion of 'the Barnacle and Ford Creek', which were apparently someone else's perquisite.[1] In 1630 (when two Wivenhoe dredgermen were accused of poaching on it) the fishery was 'letten by lease' to two 'ffarmers of the Town, dredging for oysters for certain years to come', and in 1766 it was rented to six Brightlingsea dredgermen for five years at £10 a year, a figure which had hardly changed for a century.

Two years after the issue of this lease, however, Maldon's charter was dissolved, as Colchester's had been forty years previously. When it was renewed in 1810, the new charter was much more specific as to the rights conferred, and there was a flurry of activity to make new regulations.

Members of the Corporation made a voyage round the Knoll Sand to establish their water boundaries in 1813 and again in 1836. In 1823 a more remarkable voyage was made by Commissioners appointed by the Court of Exchequer, who ruled that the port of Maldon should extend from a line between Bilmery Creek, near Tilbury, and a tree known as the Round Tree in Milton-next-Gravesend, to the entrance of 'Holy Haven', to Shoebury-ness Buoy, to the Shoe Beacon on the south-east Maplins, and thence to St. Osyth Point, 'at a distance of one and quarter miles from the said point', and so north west to Tollesbury Point, 'where the port of Colchester commences', and westward to the town of Maldon.

A jury of twelve dredgermen was appointed to frame rules and hear reports from the Water Bailiff, whose boat flew a white flag with a blue cross, at an annual Court of Conservancy held on Steeple Stone, and then adjourning to a house in Bradwell. These occasions opened with a recital of the ancient port limits quoted above, though between 1818 and 1838 the limits below the Knoll seem to have been discreetly dropped. Dredging licences were then issued at 5 shillings each (£2 for a trawl), and a few cases of poaching by Brightlingsea and Wivenhoe dredgermen were usually reported, though whether above or below 'the Rebank' is not always clear. Few prosecutions followed, the offenders being usually content to take out a licence.

In 1837, however, a test case proved a setback to the Corporation, whose Blackwater River Committee had been advertising in the London and County Press, and distributing handbills throughout Essex and Kent, warning against trespassing. The Water Bailiff boarded a Brightlingsea smack owned by Joseph Woolvett, and the Corporation issued a writ.

The case was fought on two fronts, for the secretary of the Brightlingsea Smack Committee, Thomas Jefferies,[2] also appealed to the Lord Mayor of London, relying apparently on the importance of oysters in the metropolitan market and also on his concern for the London peter-boat men. The Lord Mayor 'did not consider the rights of the Thames fishermen under my jurisdiction are deeply affected, but I shall certainly not let the matter drop'. The following month Maldon Corporation submitted its case to the

Mansion House, but the Lord Mayor decided to leave the matter to be settled in a court of law. Rather surprisingly, a retired Maldon Water Bailiff, James Lawrence, sided against his former employers, declaring that exclusive rights were never pretended till the grant of the charter of 1810. The verdict at Essex Assizes in 1840 was in favour of Woolvett, and the Corporation had to accept that its limits now ended at the Rebank.

Ultimately, in 1886, when it was involved in dispute with the Oyster Breeding Co. mentioned below, the Corporation sought counsel's opinion.[3] Mr Serjeant Merryweather prudently refrained from getting involved in any possibilities outside the estuary, and within it avoided reference to 'the creeks thereof', which might have provoked a dispute with Tollesbury and West Mersea comparable to that between Colchester and Brightlingsea in the Colne. He concentrated on the upper oyster grounds, discovering that three payments to the Corporation by 'dreggers' from Tollesbury, Tillingham and Barling had been made in the reign of Henry VIII, and a lease granted in the time of Elizabeth I. In brief his conclusion was that while the rights were clearly set out, they had been so little exercised, and 'exclusively within Rebank', that the Corporation would be ill advised to attempt to rely on them now.

The story perhaps throws light on the dispute over Colchester's claims to the Colne. Royal charters, it would seem, were generous in conferring rights, but it was up to the Corporations to assert them, and by so doing to establish their exclusivity. The difference was that Colchester used its muscle in medieval times and got its claims confirmed in 1462, while Maldon, perhaps confused and embarrassed by the sheer extent of the territory it was claiming, waited till 1880 and even after this had to depend on the cautious qualifications of Victorian jurisprudence.

By the turn of the century Maldon was content to forget about the little maritime empire with which authorities from Henry II to the Exchequer Commissioners had so liberally endowed it. A fishing licence in 1911 merely granted rights 'between the Stone Bridge at Heybridge and the western boundary of the fishery formerly occupied by the Fish and Oyster Breeding Co. Ltd.' (referred to in a later chapter). The old limits, however, continued to be respected throughout the 19th century for customs administration (though Mersea was transferred to the port of Colchester) including the registration of fishing boats, for which purpose the port of Maldon still extends as far as Leigh, though it does not now include it.

The 'Rebank' grounds had been worked, from 1811, by a somewhat mysterious company whose members were all, with three exceptions, also members of the Corporation. As no records were kept, and there is no indication of what rent if any was paid, this Company, which continued for seven or eight years, looks like a bit of sharp practice. Mayland Creek was also leased in 1826 to a group of local dredgermen headed by Joshua Francis, but was abandoned after two years as unprofitable.[4]

With these exceptions however, the company system did not reach the

Blackwater till the formation of the Fish and Oyster Breeding Co. in 1867. This perhaps belongs, along with its more important successor, the Tolles-bury and Mersea Co., to a later period, but it may be conveniently reviewed here because it introduces a character who features in many other ventures, John Smith of The Limes, Burnham, gentleman, as he liked to describe himself. Oysters were not his only interest, for he owned a shipyard and a coal business, with a fleet of huge collier barges which traded far afield, particularly to Dover.[5] A John Smith (presumably his father) in 1820 built the Coastguard Cottages at Tillingham for the Cus-toms, and also threatened to detain one of their Revenue cutters at his yard till his repair bill was paid.[6] The first of the family in Burnham is reputed to have been a coasting skipper who settled there in the eighteenth century. The firm came to an end just before the First World War, following the loss of several craft and a fire at the yard.

The Fish and Oyster Breeding Company was established with a capital of £50,000 in £5 shares, and obtained a thirty-one-year lease for 'ground between Clark's Beacon and the Rebank' at £25 a year for the first seven years and £50 thereafter, plus £2 for every boat used and a farthing per bushel of spat and brood not taken by boat. It made a promising start, spending £11,631 on stock and employing eighteen men with seven boats. This first stock spatted, but by 1876 the grounds had been cleared, at prices up to £9 a bushel, and there was no spat.[7] No dividend was paid in these nine years and the company went into voluntary liquidation in 1878, with John Smith, its chief proprietor, as liquidator. It was replaced by the Black-water Oyster Breeding Co. Ltd., with Smith as director and secretary, and in fact the old concern under a new name, but with capital reduced to £17,900 in 3,590 £5 shares of which Smith held 3,300. This lasted no longer than its predecessor, for it laid its last stock in 1888 and was compulsorily wound up in 1891 on a petition for two and a half years' unpaid rent by Maldon Corporation. Its other founding shareholders included Lord Somers and Sir Coutts Lindsay, who soon sold out.

Smith's examination in bankruptcy suggests he was either a bit of a simpleton or a smart financial operator – perhaps the latter posing as the former. He refused to answer the simplest questions, saying he had forgot-ten, did not know or 'could not charge his memory'. Asked if the Fish and Oyster Breeding Co. was dissolved to transfer its assets to the new com-pany, he replied 'That is what I understand. The capital was too large to be hanging over shareholders' heads. I am not a lawyer.' He admitted that one of the Company's two boats, *Dauntless,* said to be laid up, was in fact working on grounds hired by him in Tollesbury Creek, and when asked why he did not pay for her use explained that he had paid for four other boats working the Company's grounds, 'as no-one else would'.

The Company's grounds evidently extended beyond those leased by Maldon Corporation, for Smith was asked about the withdrawal of a grant of Crown land, which he blamed on the Corporation's bankruptcy peti-tion, calling it 'shameful'. This was the reason he was determined not to

Smacks along the Hythe at Maldon in the 1940s. These small vessels often dredged oysters on grounds in the River Blackwater.

pay his rent. 'If they had let me alone I would have gone on,' he grumbled. Finally he burst out, 'I have not charged sixpence for my services. I have lost £10,000 of my own money, and it is very cruel to bring me here like a fraudulent man.'

In the end he accepted defeat, and paid off the Company's debts, including £125 to Maldon Corporation for rent, in consideration of the dropping of any other claims against him.

Maldon town itself never became an oyster centre. Perhaps it was, like Colchester, too far up its estuary, yet, unlike Colchester, it had a fleet of oyster smacks lying along the beach below its Hythe Quay and natural conditions that would have permitted pits ashore and layings close at hand in the estuary. Probably it was just chance that no-one in the town combined the necessary interest with the required capital.

As a result, so long as memory goes, the Maldon dredgermen had to concentrate on supplying brood to other places. They had the upper reaches of the estuary to themselves and could get a living there after a good spatfall, doing no cultivation beyond keeping the ground clean by the continual plying of their dredges. Usually, however, they had to go further afield; Ted Pitt – a veteran member of one of the principal families afloat – recalls that for seven years he could earn nothing 'above Wymarks' as the Essex men called the estuary. Spending a week away in their little smacks, which were seldom over ten tons, they knew where to look outside the Colne and Blackwater enclosures – down the Wallet and up the Rays'n, in 'Manhole' under the Colne Bar, in Walton backwaters and Harwich Harbour, and in 'Shore Ends' below Smith's Burnham grounds. 'Smith didn't do much to keep his ground clean, so we sometimes used to run a dredge or two over it for him on our way up to the Roach to bring up for the night', Ted Pitt recalled.

Brood was sold by the wash while it was plentiful – Ted Pitt remembers prices as low as 1s.9d. a wash – then, when it later became scarcer, by the hundred. Some went to the Mersea laying-holders, but much was kept for the Kentish smacks which called to collect if for the Whitstable Oyster Co. and the Ham and Seasalter Co. If laid in bags on clean ground brood would last a week provided the bag was turned over every day; without this precaution the brood began to turn black and, equally important to the frugal dredgerman, the bag rotted. Several men also found it worth hiring a little strip of ground on which to grow spat up into half-ware, to get a better price, despite having no pits for winter storage.

It was a hard and hand-to-mouth way of life, unlikely to survive into the age of Social Security and the Welfare State, which had arrived when a late effort was made to organise the remaining dredgermen into the Blackwater Oyster and Seafood Co. around 1960. This was the initiative of C.A. Devall of Chelmsford who had a laying in Goldhanger Creek. A number of dredgermen took shares, but the time for such ventures was past and before the fatal winter of 1963 destroyed what stock remained the Company had sold to Associated Fisheries.

There were about seventy dredgermen in Maldon in 1890, thirty-five in 1930 and ten in 1978. The last, Michael Emmet, gave up in 1985.[8]

Wallfleet into Crouch

There was no chartered borough to contest the manorial claims to the Crouch. Even Maldon in its wildest dreams did not try to count this river among the 'waters and shoals' within its limits – though arguably it was. Instead, this great fishery, nineteen miles in length and perhaps the longest in the country, extending from 'Clay Clodds' to the Ray Sand, was possessed by the Manor of Burnham under a last grant from the Crown made before 1272.[1] From that time to the present it has been owned by one family, the Fitzwalters and their descendants, the Mildmays, whose tenants doubtless recovered their rent by granting licences for dredging and also for other forms of fishing, for some of the leases include the right to take 'floating fish'.[2]

These exclusive rights did not go unchallenged. In 1673 the fishermen of Essex brought a claim against Lord Fitzwalter that 'the river called Walfleet from Ray Sand to Clay Clodds' was common ground, 'except for certain weirs and oyster lanes'. Proceedings on this petition were heard before a Court of Admiralty at Burnham in 1676 when the Manor asserted its claim to 'the Ray Sands adjoining to Walfleet, and the soil of the north shore of Walfleet as far as the Manor of Burnham extended', and 'the Lord's Copyhold Laynes before the town', apparently accepting the rest as a free and common fishery.

This frieze of early 19th-century maps (pages 47 to 56) of the River Crouch is taken from the "Survey and Valuation of all those Oyster Laynes lying in the parishes of Gt. & Lt. Wakering on behalf of Sir John Tyssen Tyrrel Lord of the Manors by James F. T. Wiseman."

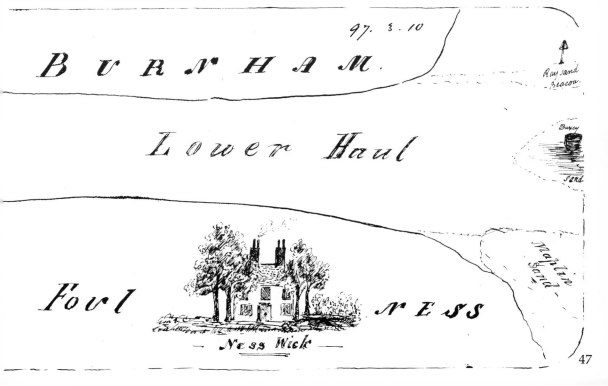

The trouble smouldered on, however, for the following year the House of Lords ordered that 'disturbances by fishermen' should be quelled by the High Sheriff of Essex, and in 1715 after further complaints that the Lord of the Manor had been 'disturbed' the offenders were ordered to be brought to the Bar of the House of Lords in custody.

At the height of these troubles, in 1686, a laying of fifty rods was leased to Sir Christopher Wren, architect of St. Paul's Cathedral, and Sir Stephen Fox, who had aided Charles II's escape after Worcester in 1651 and achieved numerous high offices. He was himself the builder of many London churches, so it is easy to see what brought the two men together, but less easy to understand why they should have decided to hire this little patch for five years at a rent of £10 a year plus four bushels of 'the said Walflete oysters'. The simplest and pleasantest explanation must be that they liked oysters.

Agreements with fishermen were in the same year made at a charge of 10 shillings plus £1 per dredge. In 1706 fishing and dredging rights were clearly distinguished, with licences to dredge 'from the east end of John Living's laying to Blacknesse', and a separate licence to a Barking man for 'floating fish, laynes excluded'.

The references to Walfleet are important because these oysters were up to the sixteenth century esteemed above all others, and historians have been inclined to credit them to the Blackwater. Norden, writing in 1594, says:

'Some part of the sea shore of Essex yieldeth the beste oysters in England, which are called Walflete oysters; so-called of a place in the

sea; but in what place on the sea it is hath been some disputation. And, by the circumstances as I have observed thereof in my travaile, I take it to be the shore which lyeth betweene St. Peter's Chappell and Crowche Creeke (The breadthe onlie of Denge Hundred), throwgh whiche, upon the very shore, was erected a wall for the preservation of the lande . . . and all the sea shore which beateth on that wall is called the Walfleet.'[3]

The Crouch at that time ran out through the Ray Sand Channel, which has since silted, as the river has preferred the more southerly exit through the Whitaker Channel. 'Walfleets' may have been dredged on St. Peter's Flats (as Norden suggests), but there seems ample evidence that they were Crouch oysters, and indeed that this was the old name of the river.

By the mid-eighteenth century the fishery began to be developed by enterprising Burnham merchants. It was leased in 1765 for six years at a rent of £120 to John Richmond, who with his son Peter was to build up a considerable trade from the Channel Islands.[4]

He was followed by Daniel Rogers, and then by five merchants, each with the Christian name John (Rogers, Auger, Sweeting, Hawkins, and Gilson) who worked in association as the Burnham Oyster Co., established in 1780. This was succeeded in 1793 by a new seventeen-year lease, at a rent of £150 to £170 a year to John Hawkins, Daniel Rogers, John Sweeting, Peter Crush and James Auger, who in 1808 had to fight another law case, costing them £1,500, to defend their exclusive rights.

The Auger family also had extensive private layings. William Auger, who died in 1876, left his to his widow, for whom they were managed by

her brother, James Auger, of Lambourne Hall, Canewdon. (The widow had apparently married another member of the same family). They comprised six acres in the Pool, four acres in 'the channel' (presumably the Roach), fourteen acres in 'Sowar-laying' and fifteen acres in 'Cliff laying'. Mr. Auger also owned six dredging boats.

These facts emerged in the course of a Board of Trade inquiry in 1882 into an application for a Several Order to establish a fishery in the Big Rill at Tillingham, a creek running across St. Peter's Flats from the Grange outfall into the Rays'n, with seven small creeks running into it. It was known as the Big Creek to the Mersea and Maldon winklers who, within living memory, anchored their little smacks there for a week while they picked the St. Peter's Flats. One can still sail a dinghy into a cut in what remains of the saltings, which a century ago doubtless extended out towards the Raysand Channel for several hundred yards. Whether there was also a deep channel outside the saltings is not clear; if so it has been flattened out of existence along with so many interesting little coastal creeks and corners swept away by tidal erosion. Whatever its exact form, the creek in 1882 had an average depth of two fathoms at low water, and was much used for dredging and eel and mullet fishing.

It sounds an improbable place to cultivate, with no shelter against easterly winds at high water, and liable to silt up, but Auger planned to spend £2,000 on cleaning it with dredges and harrows, laying culch and stocking it with French oysters, using up to six boats. He was evidently enterprising for at the time he had a steam skiff under construction, to be used for cleaning and perhaps for dredging. He explained that the lease of his farm would expire at Michaelmas and he wanted to work forty acres in the Big

Rill in addition to managing his sister's thirty acres already mentioned – a proposal which prompted an interjection from a fisherman, 'Give him the North Sea'.

The Burnham witnesses, including Peter Richmond and the deputy foreman of the Roach River Co., Stephen Argent, were all in favour, declaring that the Big Rill was little used and its development would provide employment. The Maldon and Mersea men were in opposition, putting up that peppery Colchester advocate, Henry Jones, whose verbal pyrotechnics enlivened many local inquiries and disputes at this time. He contented himself with a tirade against the new companies in general, and the Herne Bay (Kent), the Maldon Fish and Breeding Co. and the Tollesbury and Mersea Co. in particular. They were 'all failures' and it was 'monstrously unfair to take this ground away from hundreds of poor people and to place it in the hands of one or two individuals'.

Adam Howard of Mersea also poured scorn on the Tollesbury and Mersea Co., despite the fact he was its foreman, declaring that 'he did not know a foot of the Company's ground fit to take spat, because it had not been worked enough'. Another Mersea man, John Hughes (probably Hewes) claimed he had seen a hundred smacks in the Rill in a week. I have not succeeded in tracing the result of this hearing.[5]

At this time the Company owned seven smacks of from 18 to 20 tons and four smaller private smacks were also employed.[6]

For a full century the Burnham Oyster Co. continued in the hands of the Rogers, Auger, Sweeting and Hawkins families. By 1800, when the rental was raised to £1,000, it was employing 10 boats and 30 or 40 men, or at peak periods of the year up to 20 boats and 60 men, but it may then have been

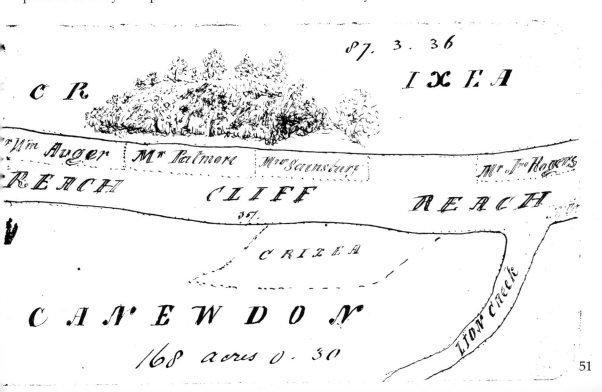

87. 3. 36

IXEA

CR

Wᵐ Auger   Mᵣ Palmore   Mrˢ Sainsbury   Mʳ Jⁿᵒ Rogers

REACH   CLIFF   REACH

37.

CRIZEA

CANEWDON

168 acres 0. 30

LION Creek

51

more a confederation than an amalgamation of the old family concerns, for when Burnham was threatened by Brightlingsea marauders at the end of the eighteenth century (as described in Chapter 13) the warning notices were published by Hawkins & Co., and when at the height of the rumpus in 1808 the Mildmay interests had to be defended at yet another costly test case, the application was undertaken by Crush & Co., who won the day but were rewarded with no more than 40 shillings damages.[7]

It was presumably the Burnham Oyster Co. or one of its constituent concerns which erected the unusual watchtower on the site of what is now the Royal Corinthian Yacht Club. Known as the Belvedere, it is marked on an eighteenth century map, was portrayed in a watercolour dated 1853, and is still commemorated by the name of Belvedere Road. This lofty lookout would have provided a commanding oversight three miles downstream to the chief fattening grounds and pits, up to Creeksea Ferry, where there were other pits, and over all the layings on the north shore of Cliff Reach. But the Company also relied on lookouts afloat; in 1863 it employed five policemen, two of them, according to the 1861 census, aboard the watch vessel *Spy,* and two more aboard Auger's 19-ton smack, *Success*. None of these were local men, a policy also followed in recruiting Customs boatmen and the members of the Colne River Police.

Since Burnham oysters were notoriously green, sales were chiefly to Whitstable for re-laying or to the Continent, but in the absence of records it is difficult to draw comparisons with the Colne and Blackwater. The annual account of the Company's affairs in Kelly's Directory refers up to the end of the century to 'Ostend, Belgium and Dunkirk' as the chief market, with the remainder going to Whitstable, but after 1900 the reference is

to Whitstable only, showing this to be the time when the foreign market was lost and dependence on Whitstable established, though some consignments were sent direct to Russia up to the First World War. Sweeting's enterprise extended to owning an oyster restaurant in London; it would be interesting to know if his customers accepted his own Company's green products.

While the Mildmay jurisdiction extended seaward as far as a transit bringing the Buxey Beacon in line with the Bradwell Chapel, the cultivated fattening grounds began just above the Roach river junction. An early nineteenth century map shows them along the north shore worked by William Auger, J. Hawkins, A. Patmore and others as far as Bridgemarsh Island, with a few cultivators on the south shore including G. Browning. Another of these layings was owned by 'the Burnham Charity' ('poor lands' endowment). Other latter-day cultivators included Cundy, who owned eight or nine smacks, several of which were bought from Whitstable, with the Kentish men sailing them as far as the mouth of the river and there handing them over to their new Essex crews. Bob Cole, who for many years ran Tucker Brown's yachtyard, recalls running away from home as a boy in 1928, after one day's experience of workshop life, to ship in Tom Yardley's smack *Fancy*. His first job was to be put with another lad in a fully loaded skiff and told to take her round to Paglesham.

While in other places smacks were almost invariably owned by their skippers, at Burnham they were mostly the property of merchants. This dated from the enclosure of the Roach in the 1860s (referred to in the next chapter), which left no common ground for 'outside' dredging and made

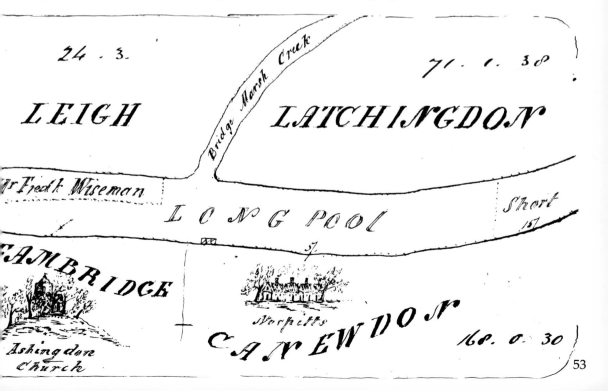

all the waters available to small smacks the exclusive preserve of the companies. In the 1870s several smacks were built by William Stebbings of Burnham for S. Addison, a development no doubt connected with the appearance in the 1890s of the name of M. Addison among the proprietors of the Burnham Oyster Company. These included the 28-foot *Mayfly*, built with her 13-foot 'foot boat', in 1877, the 28-foot *Grebe* and the 40-foot *Sea Swallow* built in 1878, and the 37-foot *Spitfire* built in 1879. Of these, the *Mayfly*, after being abandoned and bought for £24 by her builder's son for use as a motor smack, was again given a new lease of life and made a voyage round the world in 1974, when nearly a century old.[8]

Around 1905 the Burnham Oyster Co. disappeared in some sort of rationalisation or takeover, the details of which are now difficult to discover. And any reconstruction has thus to be based on references in trade directories. The Burnham Oyster Co. and its neighbour and rival, the River Roach Co. had co-existed on Burnham Quay for over a century, when in 1910 the Secretary of the Roach Co., G.L. Prussell, departed to become manager of the Colchester Oyster Fishery, where his tribulations are recounted in Chapter 14. He was replaced by J.G. Auger, Secretary of the Burnham Oyster Co. and a member of one of the founding families of that concern, which from that time on, disappears under its old name from the directories. Whatever lay behind this structural upheaval the principal lessees in the Crouch now became Smith Brothers, who comprised the sons of John Smith, Ernest and Arnold, along with their brother Witney, who took no active part. The likeliest assumption is that the Smiths merely bought out the old families – John Smith held a ten per cent shareholding as early as 1883 – but it is curious that the old name was dropped and that

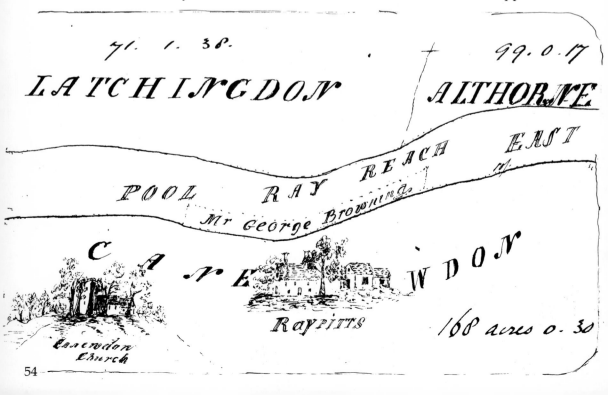

Smith Brothers does not replace it in the local directories.[9]

The Crouch went into decline during the First World War. The limpet plague seems to have struck here even harder than in the Blackwater and Colne and any extensive cultivation ended with the Second World War, despite a fine spatfall in Brandy Hole in 1947 and even though the yacht moorings were at this time still lifted annually to dredge such oysters as survived, and there was still a little activity on the grounds in the Orwell, mentioned in Chapter 9. Finally, in the 1950s, the Mildmay estate, which had suspended the payment of rent during the war, at last decided to sever that eight century old connection and dispose of the river.

Arnold Smith was now dead – the last of a long line of rugged individualists, who made the most of his deafness by hearing only what he wanted to hear in any business dealings. The periodical haggles over prices with the Whitstable buyers on whom the fishery had long become dependent were conducted on the basis that he responded to and acknowledged nothing till the minimum figure he was prepared to accept was mentioned, at which instant the deal was done.

With his passing, control was assumed by a younger member of the family, Tim Bell, who found himself faced with raising a purchase price of £8,000. This was beyond the means of a company now reduced to operating a single boat, and the answer was found in an outright sale to its chief customer, the Whitstable Oyster Co. A new company, the Burnham River Co., was established under the chairmanship of Mr. Anderson of Whitstable and the active management of Mr. Money. This carried on some cultivation till the catastrophe of 1962/3, and also recouped some of its investment by the sale of some grounds including those used for yacht moorings

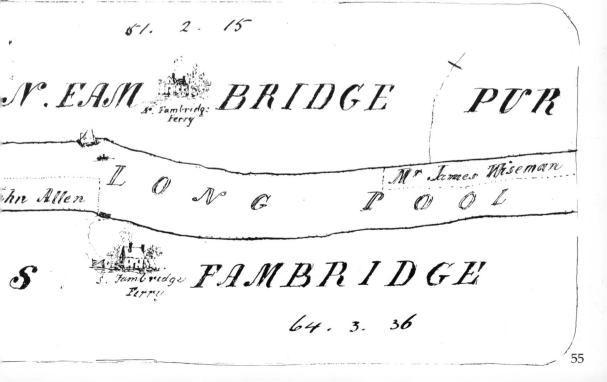

by Tucker Brown's. As a result, when the Crouch Harbour Authority was formed, it encountered many problems through the fragmentation of ownerships. Today all the yachtyards lease their moorings from this Authority with the exception of Tucker Brown.

*Working on board a steam
dredger in the River
Crouch, about 1900.*

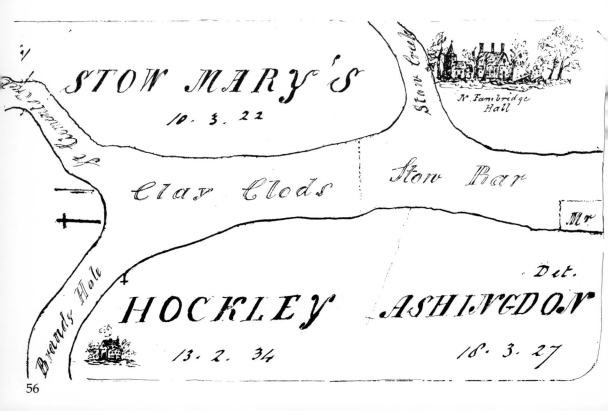

Paglesham and the Roach

The Paglesham story is particularly rich and interesting. It also introduces several personalities who appear in later chapters, making it a suitable point of departure for the exploration of the smaller oyster farms in the rivers and creeks, which were the other side of the Essex story.

The Roach enjoyed a peculiar natural advantage, for the tide did not scour through it, carrying away any suspended spat. As the Broomhill River, its upper reaches joined the Thames Estuary at Haven Gore, so the tide on the flood entered from each end, and then ebbed out in both directions. Thus spat was not washed away but checked and returned by the counter-tide. The same tidal phenomenon contributes to the success of the Loch Ryan Fishery in Scotland which has lately become the Colchester Oyster Fishery's chief supplier.

Until 1867 the river was common ground below Paglesham, with important private layings above the village and in the creeks. They were long established, for several bequests exist between 1583 and 1591 of layings and dredging 'cocks', as small boats were then locally described. One such will bequeaths forty wash of oysters along with a cock, showing it must have been made shortly before some sixteenth-century dredgerman made his last haul.[1]

Smacks racing at a Paglesham regatta in the mid-19th century.

The river layings were only edges, extending from high-water to low-water marks on the north side of Paglesham Reach. The channel and the southern shore seem always to have been common ground. This may have been because the south side belonged to a different manor, which did not see fit to lease its shore, or it may be due to natural conditions. Certainly in later years the north side was much better ground, but it is difficult to say whether this was the cause or the result of its cultivation. The layings retained their old names and a twentieth-century estate map of South Hall Farm shows those fronting its land, reading upstream from the Hard and boatyard, as Shop, Short Commons, Cokes, Ledging, Deeps, another Short Commons, Square Grounds and North Drakes. A later map, dated 1977, shows the lower half of the Square Grounds separated laterally into Black Ledge, and marks Short Commons as Common Shore and North Drakes as Broadrakes. It continues upstream with Stannets, Cutlers and Trumpions as far as Barling Hall Creek, apparently the limit of cultivation. By this time several other layings were divided laterally, with Dunhopes outside Common Shore, and two other layings outside the Ledging. There were many oyster pits in the saltings adjoining these layings, but on the south shore the only pits shown are at the upper limit of cultivation, opposite Trumpions.[2]

The creeks were all cultivated. The Pool, on the north shore just below Paglesham, was shown in the 1977 map with Rodgers at its mouth, and above this, Little Pod. The Middleway to the east of Potton Island was also worked, as was Barling Creek on the west side, where the lower grounds up to the fork were called Varletts, or The Violet, or Bullmans after a later owner.

Oyster layings at Paglesham, about 1900.

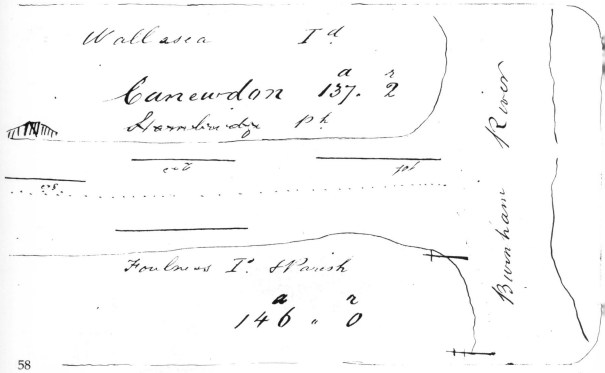

Among the holders of these Paglesham layings were the most prestigious of all the Essex oyster families, the Wisemans, who have lived in the village for over 350 years, building many of its houses and cottages and playing a leading role in the oyster trade for probably three centuries. In 1817 they were held in such esteem that the Customs were prepared to consider granting them powers of arrest in the war against Paglesham's other staple industry, smuggling, and their views were always heard with respect at the nineteenth-century inquiries recorded in later chapters. They occupied the layings nearest the Hard and boatyard, one of which was taken over about 1903 from James Wiseman, along with his home, Paglesham Chase, by Arthur Nicholls, whose son, Col. Nicholls, retained an interest in oyster cultivation till he left the village in 1940.[3]

The Paglesham merchants also showed a remarkable pioneering enterprise in the adoption of steam. The first experiment seems to have been the conversion of a sailing smack in 1842. A letter from Charles Wiseman, dated 19 May of that year and addressed to his son in Australia, tells him that 'your Uncle James and I have made a steamboat of the *Eldon*'. The engine was 3 h.p. and 'we now work in calms and all weathers'. The hull cost £100 and the machinery a further £200. She still carried a fore lug and mizzen – a curious rig but presumably the best that could be contrived with all the midships section required for boiler and machinery.

The *Eldon*'s success led to the building of other purpose-designed paddle dredgers, which can often be identified by their extremely narrow-gutted dimensions. Among the craft built by Stebbings for Addison and the Burnham Oyster Co., the 37-foot *Spitfire* had a beam of only 9 feet, with the same width across the stern. The 40-foot *Sea Swallow* was comparable, with a

Oyster layings at Paglesham, about 1900.

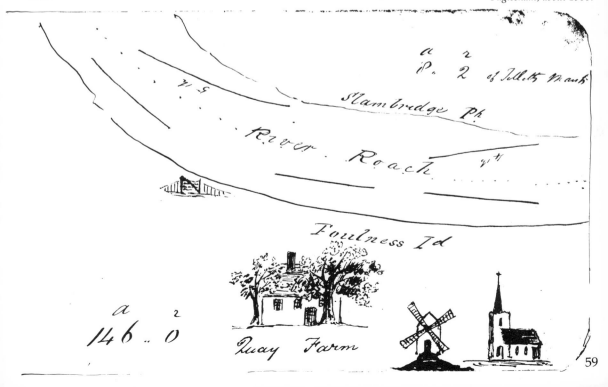

Fred and Arthur
Wiseman at their
Paglesham oyster layings,
about 1900.

beam of only 9 foot 6 inches, and she was actually lengthened by 7 feet in 1881, giving her a length of 50 feet. Later paddlers were reasonably proportioned, *Jumbo,* built by Howard of Maldon in 1882, being 47 feet long with a beam of 13 feet, or 20 feet over the paddle boxes. She became a storage hulk owned by King and Hines of Burnham in 1922. *Alice* (C.K.41) was presumably *Jumbo's* sister. Another paddler, *Victoria* (C.K. 474), also built in Maldon in 1882, was converted to motor driven propeller in 1926, with the paddle sponsons left and filled in, giving her a curiously saucer-shaped deck plan. She was owned in 1947 by Jesse Savage of Woodford Bridge, Essex. The *Firefly* was similarly converted and ended her working days at Mersea where her exceptionally long nameboard, now in the local museum, is a reminder of the broad counters favoured for this sort of hull. All these little early steam smacks, which seem to have been peculiar to the Crouch and Roach, were tiller steered, with no proper boiler or engine room, but with their primitive machinery exposed in the hold amidships. Why so many of them, and indeed so many Burnham smacks in general, were registered at Colchester with 'C.K.' numbers, instead of at Maldon with 'M.N.' numbers is unexplained.[4]

When Paglesham church was restored and largely rebuilt in 1883, the work was made possible by the generosity of James Wiseman and his fellow churchwarden, Zachary Pettitt, another leading oyster merchant who in 1870 had inherited his layings from his wife's father, George Fuller Browning, in whose family they had been for a century. During the 1880s, on the occasion of his son's twenty-first birthday party, Pettitt entertained no fewer than fifty men employed by him in the oyster industry. In 1907 he employed twenty-two men, with seven sailing boats and a steam 'launch', a description probably of wider application than today's meaning, and possibly a paddle dredger. One of his smacks, *Kate,* built for him in 1883, survives to this day.[5]

Dr. Frank Buckland, the naturalist and Inspector of Fisheries, was a close friend of the Wiseman family and leaves his name to this day in Buckland House, which in earlier times had been occupied by Susannah Wiseman, who was the grandmother of Dr. Henry Laver, for many years Chairman of the Colchester Oyster Fishery. She kept a diary which in April 1842 contains the entry: 'New steam ship proved to exceed beyond expectations', presumably referring to the family's enterprising experiments with power dredging.

Paglesham oysters were in the mid-nineteenth century largely exported to France, probably because they were green-bearded. They were, however, good enough for Disraeli, who on March 20 1874 wrote to Frederick Wiseman: 'Dear Sir, Your oysters were worthy of Roman emperors, and I have little doubt that it was these very green finned natives that impelled them to invade Britain and, I fear, conquer Essex. They were delicious, and, I am ashamed to add, I devoured most of them myself. Your obld. servt. B. Disraeli.'

The enclosure of the lower reach of the river by the Roach River Co. must have been as controversial and traumatic as that of the Blackwater a few

*Oyster layings at
Paglesham, about 1900.*

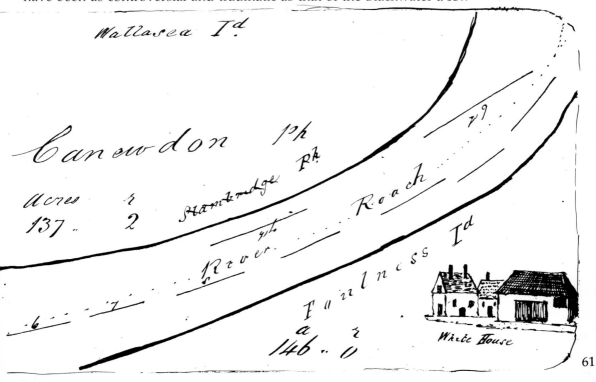

years later, but as it was decided by an Act of Parliament passed in 1864 there was no public inquiry to record the arguments for and against. At a Board of Trade inquiry in 1867, as the Company was starting operations, 'vigorous objections' were referred to in passing, and at the 'Big Rill' inquiry mentioned in the last chapter the reason the Burnham men were not interested in opposition was that since losing the Roach they had had to sell their small smacks, but these are the only hints at the passions that must have been aroused and the disruption that must have been caused by the loss of the only sheltered common dredging ground in the whole Crouch-Roach complex.[6]

Whatever the price paid by humble dredgermen dispossessed of their birthright, the new order co-existed with the old successfully for half a century. By 1867 the Company was employing forty-three men and eight boats on a square mile of ground, comprising the whole river from its junction with the Crouch up to the layings of Mr. F. Wiseman and the southern half of the river beside the layings of Mr. B. Smith and Mr. F. Wiseman. One of its first initiatives was to build up a chalk edge between the low water marks of spring and neap tides. Chalk and labour for this cost £184, and the Company also spent £451 on culch, £240 on breeding oysters, and £50 on brood and winkles. Under its chairman, W.H. Bygraves, it built up strongly over the first ten years, with sales of seventy-one bushels in 1872, rising to 862 bushels in 1875, valued at £9 a bushel. By 1870 it had sixteen pits, each forty feet by twenty feet, and was building three more boats.

Dividends were paid amounting to £2,500 (10 per cent) in 1874; £5,100 (20 per cent) in 1875 and £6,250 (25 per cent) in 1876 – a remarkable profitability, which may show the natural richness of the Roach, but probably

Oyster layings at Paglesham, about 1900.

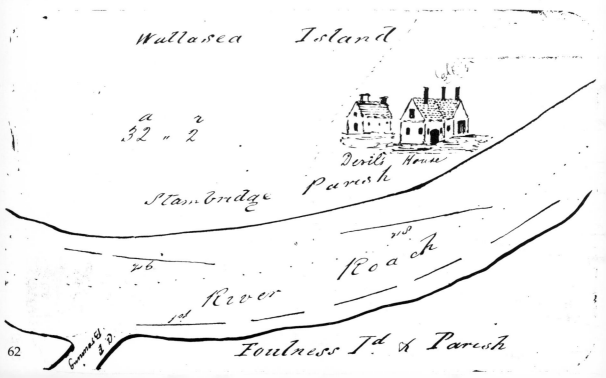

reflects also the advantages of a conventionally constituted company over those in the Colne and Blackwater, both of which were, in different ways, employee-influenced co-operatives. The Roach Co. deserved success, for it took the trouble to lay culch in two layers, with a light dressing of cockle shell spread at the critical time of spatting on to of a layer of heavier oyster shell. In 1876, 1,800 bushels of oyster shell and 1,200 bushels of cockle were used in this way.

A full comparative analysis is impossible, for the Roach Company's records were lost through the tidal flooding of a storeroom (the figures quoted are from various Board of Trade reports of the period), but it may be noted that the Tollesbury and Mersea Co., which made a less promising start in 1879, achieved sales of £12,748 in 1886 and £11,682 in 1887, while the Colne Fishery, in the first year for which sales are summarised, 1889, returned a sale figure of £10,128. The fortunes of the two latter companies are summarised in Chapters 14 and 16; it would be interesting to be able to include the Roach, but all that can be said from available evidence is that it made the strongest start of them all, and throughout the years when other companies were being asked for or established, it was usually pointed out as an example of success.

It is not clear whether the B. Smith, whose layings have been mentioned, was a connection of (or even a misprint for) the ubiquitous John Smith of Burnham, who was shown as manager of the Roach River Co. in 1869. But in 1870 it was reported that a Mr. Smith had founded a Paglesham Oyster Company, which had cleaned and culched four acres, laying sixty-five bushels of brood and halfware and fifteen bushels of grown oysters, expected to yield up to 300 bushels, valued at £2,700. 'Wherever a dredge

Oyster layings at Paglesham, about 1900.

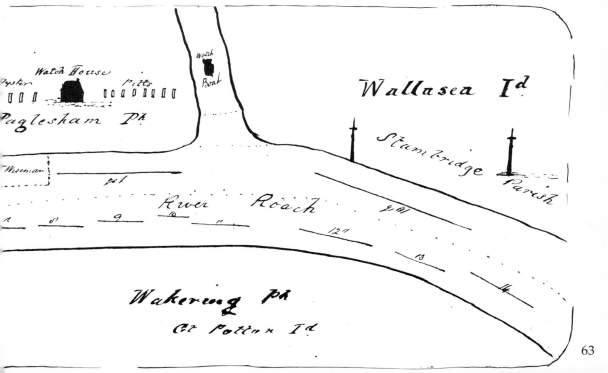

is thrown, hundreds, I might almost say thousands, of young spat are found', wrote an enthusiastic Inspector of Fisheries.[7]

By the early years of this century, the Roach River Co. was employing about 140 men and boys, with a stock of brood and halfware amounting to 14,000 tubs, averaging 1,700 to 2,000 a tub. It then had fifty pits. Its turn-over was about half that of the Colne Fishery, under a million a year, though in the 1897 boom it sold one and a half million.[8]

According to local recollection the Company continued to prosper up to the outbreak of the First World War, and then gradually succumbed to the series of difficulties and disasters which will become all too familiar in the perusal of the following chapters, finally surrendering its lease after the catastrophic winter of 1962/3, which wiped out eighty-five per cent of its stock.

The most notable attempt at revival during the decades of depression was made by Walter Keeble of Paglesham, who in 1933 took over the three lower layings on the Paglesham shore, along with the Middleway and the upper part of the Pool. After his death in 1950, his sons Hubert and Alfred carried on for another twenty years as Keeble Brothers, having to face not only the setbacks that were universal over this period but also a local disaster in 1958 when a violent thunderstorm washed tons of mud out of the rills on to the layings, smothering the oysters there.

With the Roach Co. and the old cultivators losing heart, grounds were let to a number of new tenants, some of whom made attempts to revive old glories, while some found the problems too daunting. Gilson Brothers of Southend, perhaps the most enterprising and innovative of all post-war Essex fishermen, took over most of the edges above those used by

Oyster layings at Paglesham, about 1900.

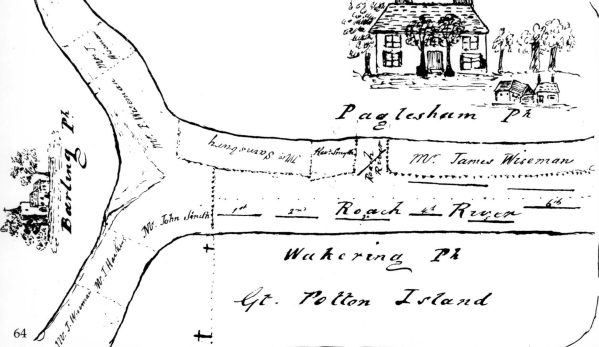

*Wintering and storage
pits on the banks of the
Roach at Paglesham.*

Keeble's, along with Barling Hall Creek, but never developed much serious cultivation. Other latter-day laying holders included Sir G. Worthington, M.C. Pipe and D. Driscoll, who held the upper reach of Potton Creek till his death in 1975. When the grounds abandoned by the Roach River Co. in 1964 were re-allocated in the 1970s, a new Burnham River Co., founded by David Duffy, with plans for cultivation on rafts, took the lower part of the Pool and ground in the river adjoining it, while the rest of the river, down to the Crouch, went to Norman Childs of Mersea, whose efforts there are described in Chapter 17, with the Ministry of Agriculture retaining a few of the old layings for its research station at Burnham.

*Oyster pits at Paglesham,
about 1900.*

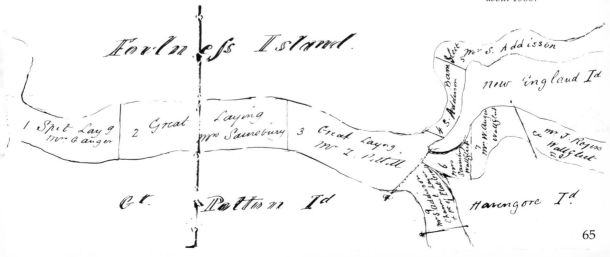

Oyster cultivation was however effectively a thing of the past when in December 1972 a Public Health Order required purification of shellfish for the Roach and the adjoining creeks. A cleansing plant was erected at the top of Barling Hall Creek by Gilsons, but this was almost entirely used for their cockle catches.

For geographical convenience and clarity the Roach River Co. has been dealt with in this account of Paglesham, but it was in fact almost entirely based on Burnham, where it had an office on the quay. It is believed that all communication was by water; there may not even have been a road from Paglesham East End down to the pits and layings. Most of the dredgermen also came from Burnham, where they were known as the Overlanders. Up to the 1920s a hundred dredgermen mustered each morning, of whom nearly half were ferried in Overland boats across the Crouch to Overland Point, opposite Prior's shipyard, from which point they trudged along the river bank to work on the Roach. The day's work finished at four o'clock, and on the return walk it was deemed prudent to keep behind the sea wall and not show one's head above it before a quarter to four. The Overland boats carried ten to twelve men, and were also used for dredging, probably by haul-tow, which is remembered at Burnham under the name 'haul-and-tow'.

As a little epilogue, we may, before saying goodbye to Paglesham, return to its golden age with a charming account left by an old Mersea resident, Sybil Brand, of her family's move there in 1909, when she was a little girl:[9]

'My father, John Brand, had been offered a foreman's job by his cousin, Horace Cooke. At Mersea the standard wage was £1 a week. We should move to Paglesham, a small village on the River Crouch, where Dad would get 35 shillings a week plus a rent-free house. Mother didn't want to leave her friends, but Dad settled that. He said 'I'm going.' Mother followed his lead. He was to be a 'working foreman', not endowed with great physical strength, but Horace Cooke knew his character. He could trust him to do his best and see that the men under him did their best. There'd been enough 'scrape, scrape' even if we did get my favourite dinner every Friday; one pork sausage, all meat, partly cooked, encased in a pastry crust.

'On a fine September morning I was hustled from my bed very early. We must catch the tide and board the *Telegraph*, James Hempstead's fifteen-ton smack, while the water was deep enough by the Causeway to get to her by rowboat in Buzzun. A bevy of aunts, uncles and cousins came to see us off. The tide wasn't big enough to get us away from the Causeway. We stuck on the mud; then back to Laurel Cottage till the next day.

'Next morning we had to start even earlier; I was roused from bed at 5 a.m. No-one came to see us off the second time. A little fair-haired girl and her mother who lived opposite parted the curtains and waved good-bye. Otherwise the morning was silent, no chimneys smoking, and only the sound of birds chirping while they searched for breakfast.

'This time we did get away. I'd never had breakfast at sea before. The cabin smelt of Stockholm tar and oilskins were piled on a bunk, but the little open stove by the mast gave out a welcome glow. We had tea and fried bacon for breakfast and all settled down for the voyage. Sailing out with the tide beyond Bradwell Point the crew kept a look-out for the Bench Head buoy, headed south for the Whitaker Channel and into the River Roach. We sailed between Foulness and Potton Island to the east and Wallasea Island to the west. Further south where the Roach narrowed we should find Paglesham.

'Later on we discovered Yoklett, the channel between Foulness and Potton yielded fine blunt soles in the trawl. My father's employer rented some oyster ground there from Zachary Pettit of Loftmans, Canewdon. Our house and all other rented ground was his or his wife's. Mrs. Pettit was the only child of a Mr. Browning, who lived in Well House, in Queen Victoria's reign and amassed a fortune from oysters. The soles were a welcome addition to our diet. Our butcher lived five miles away at Rochford and didn't call many times a week.

'We reached Shuttlewoods Hard, Paglesham, about 2p.m. Our furniture was loaded on a waggon and by permission of Mr. Nichols, of The Chase, cut across a stubble field to Well House, our new home. Only a narrow path connected us to East End, two minutes' walk away. The alternative was a mile's journey by road to reach our home from the north.

'After all the jolting we had only one breakage, a cherub in black and gold ornamenting our large hanging lamp which, with its heavy weight for raising and lowering, hung over the big table in our dining-sitting room. Mr. Cooke sent Dad a cheque for wages. I took the cheque to Mrs. Kemp of the Plough and Sail, that spotlessly clean hostelry, and took back golden sovereigns and half-sovereigns in exchange.

'We settled down at Well House with its walled garden and orchard for seven happy years. The war shattered that idyll. Oysters were too great a luxury to cultivate. We left in 1916. The seven-year lease for oyster grounds and Well House was ended.'

The Yoklett soles which so delighted Sybil Brand were in fact probably caught in the dredges, for even if they had a beam trawl, it would not have been allowed to be used on oyster ground and dredges did often in the summer yield a bonus by digging a prime sole out of the mud where he thought himself safely bedded. But this little bit of vivid recall after over seventy years seems to me a perfect cameo of what I have already referred to as the pound-a-week world of lost content.

Tollesbury and its manors

The Blackwater was a great natural nursery and source of supply for oyster cultivators far and near, but especially for those adjoining it.

Up the estuary, Heybridge and Goldhanger on the north shore and Lawling and Mundon on the south developed no oyster interests, having no creeks which were free from Maldon's control. At Bradwell there were a few layings in the creek, the ownership of which was described as 'doubtful' in 1867 when it was not known if there were any dredgermen there. At Tollesbury and West Mersea, however, creeks were under manorial jurisdiction, and these two villages developed into intensive centres of cultivation, along with Salcott Creek, though Salcott itself does not seem to have participated to any appreciable extent.

In all these places layings included the whole creek, so that the oysterman cultivated the channel bed and two edges, as described in detail in Chapter 1. Elsewhere, at Brightlingsea and in the Crouch and Roach, they were single-sided, with different owners for each edge, an arrangement which left an unmarked boundary down the middle of the channel. When Cassell French hired a laying above Burnham he found his outer boundary supposedly defined by a pair of metes in the saltings where the river curved to allow them to be placed, but often it was hardly possible to see them. All layings were usually measured by their length – sometimes as little as eighty or 100 yards – without reference to breadth, though occasionally grounds are referred to by acreage.

Tollesbury Creek was until comparatively recent times divided into a north channel and a south channel. In the upper part of the creek this division is still marked by Cob Island (though not for much longer, if erosion continues at its present pace), but lower down the creek another little island has vanished, along with the mud spit formerly connecting it with the end of Cob, locally known as 'Flaxy' (perhaps a memory of the William Flack mentioned below). As recently as the 1950s the Tollesbury shrimpers had to grope their way up the south channel, because if they took the wider north channel there was not enough water over the submerged middle ground for them to reach their anchorage at Woodrope Creek. Today the whole creek is a wide, featureless expanse, becoming part of the Blackwater estuary with the erosion of the Nass shoal, which forty years ago was a-dry at half-ebb. Yet in the medieval setting-out of the layings, the distinction was so clear that those in the north channel belonged to the Manor of Tolleshunt Gynes, and those in the south channel to the Manor of Tollesbury Hall, which, in 1867, included 54 layings.

The manorial system was as decoratively anachronistic as a heraldic coat-of-arms, certainly for the last two centuries of its operation and *Tollesbury and its* perhaps for twice that time, but its formalities continued to be observed. *manors* The financial demands were not extortionate, the quit-rent being often a few wash of the best oysters, later transmuted to 10 shillings a year, or the lawyers' favourite 6s. 8d. Many deeds continued to show the old and new alternatives up to the end of the nineteenth century, but there is no way of guessing how long the medieval payment in kind actually persisted. The copyhold layings could be freely bought and mortgaged and could probably even have been auctioned, with some legal proviso of acceptability to the lord of the manor, but this form of sale was rarely, if ever, practised up to the end of the nineteenth century. The bills of sale proclaimed themselves as 'The General Baron of the Lord of the said Manor', and went on to describe how 'the customary tenant came before me, the Deputy Steward' for 'the purpose of making and passing the absolute surrender' of a laying 'out of his hands into the hands of the Lord of the said Manor, by the rod'. The new tenant was then 'admitted and his fealty is respited', often by the payment of a fine. When a tenant died in 1774, 'who was his heir the said Homage knew not', so 'proclamation was made three times after the custom of the said Manor, but no-one came'.

In fact the 'General Court Baron' probably consisted of a visit to a solicitor approved by the manor and with a knowledge of the jargon. A conveyance of 1902 gives the game away, for the black-letter heading 'Manor of Tolleshunt Gynes otherwise Tolleshunt Bourchiers' then reads on 'in the county of Hertfordshire', instead of the usual 'county of Essex'. It was prepared by a solicitor in Hertford, who presumably felt the court had moved into his office! It would be interesting to know how often a lord of the manor exercised his theoretical right to reject an occupier and how the fines paid on conveyance were fixed, for they varied without explanation or apparent rhyme or reason from a few pounds up to £50, and were sometimes marked 'by special favour'.

The end of this system began with the Copyhold Act, 1894, and various Ministry of Agriculture and Fisheries Acts, 1889 to 1914, but many of the oyster cultivators in the manors mentioned were in no hurry to claim their freedom, perhaps because they had to pay for it. By the 1920s, however, enfranchisement was being enforced by the Ministry of Agriculture and Fisheries. The enfranchisement of the Harryard layings, mentioned below, cost the new owner £65 in 1919.

The deeds of three layings in the north channel go back to 1664. In 1744 John Kempton of Mersea occupied the upper laying, 'formerly in the occupation of Christopher Howsett', and the middle and lower layings 'formerly occupied by William Trayler and Samuel Hall'. His sale in that year to William Smythies of Colchester, surgeon, is witnessed by John Hawes and Thomas Criswick, also tenants. From 1835 to 1854 they were occupied by Thomas and John Sanford, the Wivenhoe merchants already mentioned, who were succeeded by three generations of the Bartlett family, the

69

last of whom, William Bartlett, worked them into the 1930s with his pretty little smack *Sprite,* sailing from Wivenhoe on a Monday and returning on Friday, setting a topsail (unusual in a small dredging smack) and disdaining an engine to the end.

On two occasions layings in this Creek were restored 'at great trouble and expense', one by Samuel Woolvett in 1830, and one adjoining it by Charles Cox in 1859. Both had their enterprise rewarded by being admitted to the Manor for a nominal fine of one shilling.

In the south channel the layings were called the Harryards, Hallyards or Hall Yard, 'formerly Shaw King's'. They were sold in 1809 by Henry Hawes to William Willett of East Donyland and Daniel Sutton, the notorious Colchester Town Clerk described in *The Smugglers' Century.* On Willett's death in 1850 they passed to Thomas Wallis, a Northumberland ship builder, who sold next year to T. J. Jefferies for £54. After passing through other members of this Brightlingsea family they were bought by G. Harvey for £176 in 1876 and were still owned by his descendants when they were enfranchised in 1919.

Salcott Creek fell under yet another jurisdiction, the Manor of Great Wigborough with Salcott. It was commonly called 'The Great Dyke', a name also used for Mersea Fleet, but in this case needed to distinguish it from 'Little Ditch'. The eighteenth-century occupiers have been referred to as members of the Protection Association. Among them Thomas Overall's ground passed to Charles Southgate and then in 1851 to Thomas Harvey. It was then described as abutting on one side on a laying formerly occupied by George Barrington and then William Frost, and on the other side by a laying formerly occupied by Anne Bragge, then John Balls, then Robert Sadler. Harvey bequeathed it in 1886 to his son-in-law, Herbert Pryor, along with a laying in Tollesbury North Fleet, abutting on one side on a laying 'formerly of Uriah Clark' and on the other side the laying reclaimed by Samuel Woolvett and 'formerly occupied by Francis Lucking'.[1]

In the 1880s, the layings in Tollesbury north and south channels belonging to George Harvey, 'of West Mersea, late of Wivenhoe', along with those in the Colne Geedons Creek were formed into the Colchester Native Oyster Fishery Co. Ltd., with a capital of £50,000 in 10,000 £5 shares. With 30 acres of ground, covering three miles in length, it ranked in importance only behind the Colne and T. & M. companies, according to its secretary, George Wittey, a Colchester lawyer.[2]

Harvey was a big customer of the Tollesbury and Mersea Co., buying half a million oysters at the high price of 10s. 6d. a hundred in 1885. He was also a slow payer and several times annoyed the Company by dumping culch on its Old Hall saltings. In 1886 a legal action (unspecified) between him and the T. & M. was settled with £25, both parties withdrawing their claims and the Company paying him. The directors of the Colchester Native Oyster Fishery Co., in addition to Harvey, included Claude Egerton

Green of Wivenhoe Hall, George Harvey of Abberton, Major Tyssen Holroyd of Donyland Lodge and J. Algernon Ind, of Whitehall, Colchester. The shareholders included Horace Egerton Green and Charles Gurney Hoare, who were partners in the Norwich bankers, Gurney, Round, Green and Co., which advanced money for the formation of the Oyster Company. This bank became part of what is now Barclays Bank in 1836, with two of its directors, Sir Eustace Gurney and Edward Gurney Buxton, purchasing the Tollesbury layings for £500.

The Native Oyster Fishery Co. seems to have been short-lived. By 1901 Somerset House was demanding an overdue annual return from W. Stammers of Brightlingsea who, as has been mentioned, sold the Geedons to Colchester Corporation in the same year. Perhaps this was the end, for in 1908, when the middle and lower layings were sold by the Bartletts of Wivenhoe to Charles Gurney Hoare for £362, they were described as adjoining the layings of 'the late Colchester Oyster Fishery Co.'.

This Norfolk banking connection also seems to have extended into another shadowy concern, the Stag's Head Oyster Co. of Norwich (invariably and libellously referred to at Mersea as the 'Bogus Company') for a lease was signed on its behalf in 1944 by D. G. Buxton, a local director of Barclays' Norwich Office. This was to hire the layings of Hector Cooke of Mersea, in Salcott Creek, 'formerly of John Storey and Francis Butcher, lying between a laying formerly of Thomas Criswick and later of William Howard, Sen.', and a 240-yard laying 'formerly occupied by Hugh Baker'. The lease at £50 a year was two years later sold to Bentley's Oyster Fishery Co. Ltd. of Clacton, the enterprise of William and Derek Bentley, proprietors of Bentley's London Oyster Bars. The Bogus Company operated in the Tollesbury north channel.

Tollesbury also had its own oyster company, established in 1845, with a capital comprising 500 £32 shares. At the first annual meeting, held at the Plough and Sail, the chairman, H. May of Maldon, reported that several grounds had been engaged and £2,000 worth of brood deposited. These grounds included part of the river, 'between Bradwell and Maldon, above Stansgate', where in 1846 the Company was asking the Customs for immediate clearance of a freight of Jersey oysters. But the enterprise lasted only till 1851. Its first secretary, Robert Solly of Mundon, who owned a yacht and was a member of the Royal Thames Yacht Club, resigned after a year, and told the first Blackwater inquiry in 1867 that the Company spent £4,500 in three years, after which it was valued at £500. He also mentioned on that occasion that Tollesbury had 30 dredgermen, with 80 boats worth £100 each.[3]

CHAPTER
EIGHT

The Mystery of Mersea's Creeks

The West Mersea oyster grounds were part of the Manor of West Mersea, whose first rights were granted by Edward the Confessor to the Priory of St. Ouen in 1046. Little is known of their early history, but by the eighteenth century the May family were Lords of this Manor, the last to hold the title being Henry John May, who in 1887, after the estate had been broken up, made over the waterside interests to his grandson, Willoughby John Bean.[1] The process of enfranchising began in the time of Henry May's father, who died in 1843, and was completed, with a few exceptions, in a sale by auction in 1914. The 'Little Ditch' Creek, connecting Thornfleet and Salcott Fleet, was part of the Manor of Great Wigborough and Salcott, and was similarly enfranchised in 1922, when C.J. Wilkin of Tiptree was Lord of the Manor.

This evolution from medieval to modern times was confused by a bizarre complication. In 1667 Charles II made a grant of the Mersea creeks to the Charterhouse, the London hospital and school which later developed into the public school in Surrey. This grant, which gave power to enclose the creeks (whether by damming them completely or inwalling their saltings is not stated), remained forgotten for nearly three centuries till in the 1960s the owner of New Hall, Little Wigborough, Victor Gray, found the entitlement among his deeds and set out to exercise the rights he claimed, including the ownership of the beds and foreshores of the creeks, a claim which the Crown Estates Commissioners accepted as a better title than theirs.

The challenge to the oyster fisheries culminated in 1967 in a claim for damages against Cassell French and his son Peter for planting oysters on their layings in the Strood Channel.[2] Proceedings were stayed indefinitely before this case came to court, but Mr. Gray returned to the attack two years later, claiming trespass damages and injunctions restraining the Frenches from planting oysters on the foreshore. The application failed, with the County Court judge awarding costs against Mr. Gray.[3] The boatyards and the West Mersea Yacht Club, however, formed a company to purchase from Mr. Gray the rights he claimed over the yacht anchorage, and this consortium, known as Mersea Haven Ltd., continues to claim payments from the owners of moorings to this day.

One happy result of this unhappy period of threat, counter-threat and impending litigation was that the Mersea layings are now unusually fully documented, thanks largely to the labours of Cassell French, who devoted several years of his retirement, and risked the rewards of many years of his working life, on the defence of this birthright.[4]

At the time of Mr. Gray's actions, which coincided with the last years of general cultivation and the start of the decline caused by the disastrous winter of 1962, there were seven layings in the Strood Channel, which had been greatly improved during the 1880s by Elijah Cooke, who hardened the edges with barge-loads of chalk, and who after his death and that of his son was succeeded by Willoughby Bean, who owned the ground and worked it himself till the sale in 1914 already referred to.[5] In Mersea Fleet, between Packing Marsh Island and Cobmarsh Island, there were four layings,[6] while Buzzen Fleet had one laying owner,[7] and Little Ditch was divided into no fewer than 15 layings.[8] These layings were all measured by their length, which was sometimes as little as 50 or 100 yards, without any regard to their breadth, and were marked off by withies and signboards. At this time no fewer than 200 oyster pits, used and abandoned, can be counted on maps of the area.

The mystery of Mersea's creeks

A point of some interest is that there were no layings in Thornfleet and the Ray Creek till these were awarded to the Tollesbury and Mersea Co. in the late nineteenth century. The explanation seems to be that this channel, once called 'Middle Ditch and Peldon alias Thorn Fleet' was not in existence at the time of Charles II's grant in 1667, let alone in the Middle Ages when many of the layings were doubtless first laid out and leased, but was

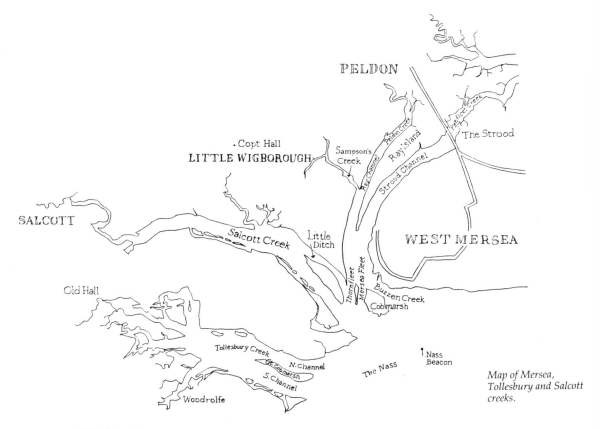

Map of Mersea, Tollesbury and Salcott creeks.

formed by the inwalling of the Feldy marshes from Sampson's Creek down to the junction with Tollesbury Creek in the latter half of the eighteenth century. Before this time the tide ebbed and flowed over hundreds of acres of saltings, through which 'Middle Ditch' ran as a small channel only a few feet wide. The new walls directed the tide into this stream and scoured it out to create the Thornfleet and Ray Creeks known today.

There were thus only two entrances, instead of the three familiar in modern times – Buzzen and the 'West Mersea and Great Ditch' as it was called in 1667.[9] At its south end this did not follow the course of the present Mersea Fleet, for Cobmarsh and Packing Marsh were then one island, with the 'Great Ditch' flowing to the west of it and joining the Buzzen above it at a point where there is reputed to have been a causeway from the shore to the island.[10] All the old maps,[11] up to and including the great Chapman and André survey published in 1777, but surveyed some years before, provide supportive evidence, showing a single creek winding up to the Strood. This creek was called 'Pyefleet Creek and Mersea River' in 1815, 'Mersea Channel' in 1777 and 'North Fleet' in 1778. The name Pyefleet is confusing, but perhaps recalls a memory of the time when the Strood was a lower dividing barrier and the Pyefleet was thought of as a single creek joining Colne and Blackwater behind Mersea Island.

There are a number of glimpses of life in this oyster world in bygone days. In 1700 one John Pottle, owner of a laying, fell ill and the Overseers (the trustees of the Church Strood Lands) gave him money and other help, usually a bag of flour and firewood. He did not recover, and on his death the Overseers seized the oysters on his laying, selling 20 bushels to a Dutch buyer at 8 shillings a bushel.[12]

A detailed picture of the Mersea layings at the end of the eighteenth century can be gained from the records of a Protection Association, which was started in 1789 and lasted till 1829.[13] The original intention was to include Brightlingsea, Wivenhoe and Tollesbury, but after two years the usual parochial jealousy seems to have arisen, for these places are struck out in a surviving copy of the articles of association. The first members, however, include William and Benjamin Sanford of Wivenhoe, already mentioned, who with their 21 layings and three boats were the biggest operators. Eleven Brightlingsea members owned 72 layings, and at Tollesbury three members owned nine.[14]

At Mersea John Braisted was the largest owner, with 24 layings, while others include Thomas Steven and Samuel Overall, William and John Brand, John Barrett, Bennet Hawes (the Association's treasurer), William Haward, Uriah Clarke, John Simpson and Francis Lucking. Of these names only the Hawards have remained in the trade up to modern times, though the Brands were prominent into the present century. Uriah Clarke's connection if any with the present Mersea family is not known. Otherwise the names so familiar in the trade, including French, Mussett, Stoker and Banks have yet to make their appearance, though a James

French was in membership in 1825 with a laying in 'the Fleet' – probably the ground in Strood Channel worked by his family up to the 1980s – and a Mussett appears in 1829.[15]

The location of the Mersea layings was precisely set out in 1807. There were nine in the Fleet below the Causeway, seventeen in Salcott Fleet, seven in 'Dyche' (Little Ditch), eight in the Fleet above the Causeway and five in Tollesbury Creek. The Causeway refers not to the present boat jetty, but to an old walkway reputed to have connected the north end of Packing Marsh Island to the shore near the present day Victory Hotel. The Salcott layings are differentiated as being above and below the sluice, and sixteen 'marshes' are listed, perhaps meaning shore pits. The Buzzen Creek is not mentioned till 1824 when James Mussett makes his first appearance with one laying, one boat and one marsh in 'The Busson', worked by his descendants till recent times.

Subscriptions were levied at the rate of two shillings in the pound on the 'rentable' value of the layings, plus four shillings a boat. This raised £33 in 1798 but as activity increased and the 'foreign' membership dropped out the rate rose as high as ten shillings in the pound. At first the members kept their own watch, receiving three shillings a night. A watch house was built in 1808 and a full time watchman appointed in 1818. When anything suspicious was detected he was joined by two others, one of them a member of the Association. Payments of three shillings a night are justified by a note: 'Had they not been out it appears to have been William Cutts' and John Larkin's intention to rob S. & W. Overall's ledgings, they having several baskets in their punt, and oysters had been shovelled out of the ledgings and shot in again in heaps.'

Attendance at meetings was enforced by a fine of 2s. 6d. for absence 'unless prevented by sickness or by being at sea', but in 1813 perhaps things

Oyster packing shed and pits at West Mersea, before 1914.

75

were getting out of hand, for it was decided that 'instead of meeting to dine annually to settle the accounts of this Association a meeting shall be held on the evening after Lady Day and every member shall pay his own reckoning instead of one guinea being paid out of the fund.' This guinea allowance had been agreed in 1810, and the following year the members also approved '3s. to Mr. King for three glasses of punch Thomas Brand had the night they caught James Cook'.

The first successful prosecution was that of John Pearce, who got a three-month sentence for stealing from Bennet Hawes' laying in Tollesbury Creek in 1790. In the same year Frederick Nicholson detected his father's apprentice stealing his oysters. In 1809 two Maldon men were charged with trawling in Salcott Creek but acquitted at Quarter Sessions. Four Harwich men were sent to prison for two months for stealing from William Haward senior, but had their penalty mitigated after one of them, William South, assisted the keeper of the Colchester Bridewell when other prisoners tried to escape. James Cook of Salcott was a constant offender. He was seen in August 1809 working on Bennet Hawes' laying but was acquitted. Two years later he was seen by Thomas Brand and J. Tansley dredging on Brand's laying in Salcott. This time the judge told him he was liable for seven years' transportation but 'in mercy' he would be sentenced to only twelve months' hard labour. In 1802 John Cadman was in trouble for running his barge up Salcott Creek too early on the tide and grounding on a laying. (This was also a constant source of friction between shipping and oyster interests in the Colne.) He was excused prosecution on payment of 10s. 6d. expenses and four shillings for an advertisement in the *Chelmsford Chronicle* acknowledging his fault. Anchoring on the layings in Salcott was

Loading culled and packed oysters into a skiff from a packing shed, West Mersea, before 1914.

also opposed. There were a great many boats there in September 1819. 'All *The mystery of* were very civil except a man by the name of Bunn who didn't know they *Mersea's creeks* could hinder him anchoring on the layings.'

Though the Association's affairs continued to be recorded up to 1820 there must have been some lapse or breakdown thereafter, for in 1824 the merchants 'resolved for the better security of their property from depredation to form an Association'. Though the previous Association is not mentioned, the same record book was used, so this was evidently in fact a revival.

It was agreed to purchase a boat, to be kept moored for the accommodation of the watchman, who was paid sixteen shillings a week with £5 reward payable to him or any other informant for a conviction. Members agreed to take turns in visiting the watchman 'at least once a week' for a payment of 2s. 6d. and no-one was to be 'admitted into the company for shipping oysters into foreign and other vessels if they refused to subscribe to the articles of this Association'. This is the only known mention of a company for the export of oysters. There is, however, a reference to the practice in 1829, when John Hubbard, a former watchman, was charged his 'quarter subscription' of 6s. 3d. and then the same amount again 'for Goodwin's laying because he would put the oysters into the Dutchman'.

In 1826 it was ruled that the watchman should not go below Tollesbury Fleet, fishing or with freights. He was not to go ashore until the people were at work and was to be off again by the time they leave. And he was not to be ashore but three whole days in each week.

The last recorded prosecution was in 1826. Thereafter the Association seemed to have come to an end, possibly because at this time coastal protection was improved with the introduction of the coastguard. A few items of expenditure added on the last page suggest that a balance in hand was being used up. Most are for routine upkeep of a punt but one, dated April 8, 1831, reads: 'For the boys being placed in the Cage five shillings.'

Leigh, Harwich and Ipswich

Outside the three great estuaries, the chief Essex centre of oyster cultivation, in terms of output, or perhaps through-put, was Leigh and its neighbour Southend.

The right to fish in Hadleigh Ray dates back to 1220, when Henry III conferred it on his justiciar, Hubert de Burgh, the builder of Hadleigh Castle. The right reverted to the Crown on several occasions, and by lease or purchase has been held by many people, till in 1936 it was transferred from the Salvation Army to Southend Corporation.[1]

There are also records of layings at Southchurch, precursor of the modern Southend, dating back to 1381.[2] Apparently, however, cultivation had died out by the early eighteenth century, when the virtues of the shore were discovered as a result of an accident, vividly described by Morant.[3] Writing in 1768 he says:

'About the year 1700 one Outing, having been out at sea in his hoy or boat, and having on board some small oysters more than could be used, he threw them overboard on this shore. About a year after, being accidentally here at low water and seeing these oysters, he opened some and found them much improved in size and fatness. He got more oysters and tried the experiment again, and found it to answer. Upon that, he went to Mr. Asser and took a lease of this shore at a low rent, the method of improving oysters by laying them here not being known. By this trade, Outing got a great deal of money and built a house near the sea, now inhabited by a dredger. From that time advantageous leases have been granted of this shore, and a great trade in oysters here carried on.'

The tale is taken up in the commonplace book of a gossipy Essex surveyor, John Lee, describing the growth of the Prittlewell Shore Co., 'which still continues, and at an advanced rent of 150 from 100 pounds a year, which before Outing came was nothing at all . . . it employs a great many hands, by land and water.' Lee thus describes cultivation on the mud flats:

'When the tyde is out men put on long sea boots, and walk to them, a mile or two, or three, and pick them up by hand, at so much a wash, nay, by moonshine, and put them into a large boat, set upon the shore on purpose, and may, if they mind their business make two tydes a day and earn a good deal. And besides all that, in the year 1725, there was not a house of any sort, upon the shore, at Southend, in Prittlewell, and now by the oysters being laid there, is a rowe of six or seven good houses, and one with good accommodation and fireing, which the oyster pickers, that go down upon the shore, cannot do without, to put on and off their dirty wet sea boots, once, and often twice a day as the tyde happens.⁴'

According to Lee, Outing bought oysters from Poole and Cancale; 'every bushel did not cost above three shillings, laid down; and measured out more than two bushels at Billingsgate, and seldom sold for less than eight or nine; a fine profit, in so short a time.'

The adjacent Prittlewell shore was also described by Morant as 'a good nursery' stocked from Sussex and Dorsetshire layings. He adds:

'The owners of the oysters here have their proper limits staked out, and have an advantage over the rest of the dredgers of this county in being so much nearer London, but, in a frosty season, the oysters here, from the shallowness of the water, are more liable to be killed by the severity of the weather; the shore being even, and dry when the tyde is out, and not having the conveniency of the pits and layings about Colchester and Maldon, which are replenished with new water almost at every tyde'.

In 1728 a well-known Leigh resident, Isaac Lambe, paid rates for layings on the Chalkwell shore, followed by none other than Thomas Lee, the narrator of the yarn just told, but the trade reached its peak in the 1850s when Chalkwell, part of the Swatch and Leigh Creek, was held by a London firm, Alston and Austin, who fought off the efforts of the Crown to dislodge them. Dating back, as we have already seen, to the eighteenth century, they had their own fleet of smacks, bringing oysters for re-laying from Jersey, Ireland, Wales, Cornwall and Norfolk. A Leigh merchant, John Plumbe, also employed the coasting sloop *Good Intent* to bring in oysters from Jersey and France.⁵

Rail transport to London became available in 1855 and in that year no less than 467 tons of oysters were despatched, along with twenty-nine tons of mussels, winkles and shrimps. Nine years later the total for oysters and shrimps had risen to 704 tons – nearly two tons a day – and this was in addition to the trade by water to Billingsgate, where Mayhew, writing in 1864, describes the long row of oyster boats along the wharf, called by the costermongers 'Oyster Street':

'On looking down the line of tangled ropes and masts, it seems as if the little boats would sink with the crowds of men and women thronged together on their decks. Each boat has its black signboard and salesman in his white apron walking up and down his 'shop'. "Who's for Bakers?", "Who's for Archer's?", "Who'll have Alston's?" shout the oyster merchants, and the red cap of the man in the hold bobs up and down as he rattles the shells about with his spade'.⁶

Yet only a few years later, in 1872, this whole fishing trade had been abandoned, with the grounds given over to winkles and a few mussels – presumably as the result of pollution from growing Southend, or the filth discharged from the L.C.C.'s new outfalls at Barking and Crossness and dumped in solid form by barges. In 1903, however, there were still three layings in Hadleigh Ray, owned by Baxter & Sons, G. Hammond and T. Wright, despite the fact it had also attracted Dr. Bulstrode's suspicion.

The offshore layings developed by Outing lasted till the poisoning scare of the 1890s, when those to the east of Southend Pier were passed as safe, but those to the west were condemned. Six 'obnoxious' floating boxes – doubtless the answer to the lack of storage pits mentioned in 1700 – were scrapped, and then Baxter & Sons decided to close all the layings, removing the stock to Colemouth Creek in the Medway till the Southend Corporation's sewerage scheme was completed. In 1912 the last of the local oyster and mussel trade was still affected by the incomplete works.

In 1725, soon after their establishment or revival, these Southend layings were raided by Kentish men; Lee's account of this spectacular affray will be found in Chapter 13.

At Harwich, oysters were, around 1730, 'caught in the sea before this haven but in no plenty'[7] but the town failed to establish its claim to them in 1744, when some Brightlingsea smacks dredged four bushels valued at seventeen shillings. The Harwich men boarded the smacks and seized back the oysters, but in the test case that followed the Corporation did not succeed in establishing an exclusive right. 'Oyster lays or pits, late in the occupation of Mr. Robert Living' were advertised to be let in 1750, 'in the creek between the Ray and Dovercourt', perhaps stocked from 'Mr. Living's laying in the Crouch,'[8] and the trade was remembered in an old jingle, recalling that in the busy harbour all sorts of jetsam came up in the dredge, for a day's catch was described as:

> A wash of great and a bushel of small
> A silver buckle and a two-headed maul

One of the problems was that Ipswich exercised maritime rights over the harbour – a long-standing local grievance. In another test case in 1805 Ipswich Corporation attempted to prevent unlicensed dredging there, with the Mersea Oyster Association referred to elsewhere joining in the opposition to such protection. But the Ipswich application failed, and the Harwich grounds were soon dredged out by those who had obtained the freedom to do so.

The harbour master told the Tidal Harbours Commission in 1845 that 'we used to have a great deal more spat than now, particularly about the Gristle [a sandbank dredged away soon after this date], and Shotley Ferry. I have, many years ago, seen fifty sail of smacks in the harbour, dredging for spat, which they took to Brightlingsea. The Harwich people frequently grumbled about it'.

William Groom, the smack-owner, suggested that layings in the Stour, from Shotley Gate, to Erwarton Ness, might be very profitable, and in 1863 three miles of ground between Erwarton and Stutton were leased by one

Michael Willis, 'a gentleman who has lately taken a lively interest in Harwich.' He announced the formation of the Stour Oyster Fishery, promising to start operations at once. A few months later he held another meeting, declaring that the project was 'going on very satisfactorily' and was not 'a myth or political dodge'.

The following year his manager, Harry Russell, told the Royal Commission on Sea Fisheries that he had been unable to obtain brood, but had stocked the fishery with ware and halfware from Ireland, laid in fifteen to eighteen feet of water as a precaution against frost. Willis's lease expired in 1870, when the fishery was advertised to be let by the Commissioners of Her Majesty's Woods. Whether it found a new tenant, and whether it operated up to that date, I have not discovered, but in 1867 Russell, now described as Captain Russell, appeared at a Maldon inquiry representing the Herne Bay Co. Asked about the Stour by the Clerk to the Colne Fishery (Mr. Goody) he replied, 'We had a lease but Mr. Goody said he would send boats to take the oysters away'. He then alleged that Goody had threatened to send 'a fleet of Brightlingsea smacks' to take oysters from the Orwell, with which he seems also to have been connected.[9]

Ipswich itself had a fishery of particular interest, due to the detail and unusual features of its early records.

In 1580 full-time dredging was confined to Lent, and forbidden from May to August inclusive. In other months out of Lent, it was permitted 'only once a week, viz. on Thursday', with the charitable exception already mentioned in the account of 'summer dredgers'. It was ordered that every dredgerman 'shall after every hale cull his oysters before he hale again', and 'shall take away only suche as are faire growne'. All oysters had to be sold at 'the Common Key', and 'noe person shall bring oysters to market that have above two on a cluster'.[10]

In the mid-eighteenth century Thomas Tunmer was advertising 'own country oisters, at Bourn Bridge, Ipswich, from the head fishery, 2s. 0d. per hundred and 3s. 0d. per bushel, at the pit's mouth'.[11]

But the trade seems to have died out when in 1853 the town decided to establish a fishery in the Orwell, in the hope it would rival Colchester. The Corporation granted a twenty-one-year lease for the whole river from Stoke Bridge to Shotley the following year to the town's chief shipbuilder, named (by coincidence) William Colchester.

'An Act . . . for regulation and improvement of the Oyster Fishery in the River Orwell within the Boundary of Ipswich' in 1859 introduced byelaws specifying that boats must be of four to twenty tons, and must take only one wash a day unless authorised by the bailiff. A licence system was operated, with Freemen paying £1 for four dredges and non-Freemen £2; all oysters to be handed to the watchboat. Oysters were brought from West Mersea, Harwich Harbour, Orford and Whitstable, and despatched to Newmarket, East Bergholt and Stowmarket. In 1863 eleven boats were at work, but by 1866 the fishery had accumulated a loss of £1,640 through 'insufficiency of balance of sale monies to pay working expenses and interest on money borrowed', including a loan of £6,000 from Watts, the Harwich ship-owner.

The 1859 Act was therefore followed in 1867 by an Enlargement Act, to enable a lease to be granted, and in 1873 the fishery was leased for twenty-four years to the Ipswich Oyster Fishing Co. Ltd., which took over Watts's £6,000 mortgage and employed half a dozen smacks belonging to him.

William Colchester was awarded £1,165 for his loss, but it is not clear if he continued in the new company. The manager in 1870 was J.W. Jolly, who one starlit night was keeping watch when he heard the splash of a dredge, and was able to secure a conviction against three Brightlingsea stone-dredgers trying for an easier and more rewarding harvest.[12]

Rum to the value of seventeen shillings was also given to the coastguards at Pin Mill and Harwich for assistance with watching. Around this time a Mr. Gibbs at Pin Mill Hard was granted an exceptional right to retain his laying, 100 yards long and 25 yards wide, leased at 2s. 6d. per annum.

In the 1890s the Ipswich Company had a storage pit and a wintering pit on Shotley Marshes and also dug pits on the Trimley Marshes on the advice of a West Mersea expert – only to have to close them after a short time as the result of a health scare. They could still be clearly seen till they were covered by an extension of Felixstowe Dock in the 1970s.[13]

By this time (the 1890s) the Company was mostly dealing in foreign re-laid stock. Such natives as were dredged were sold immediately, and with little spat the grounds were 'at a discount'. The fishery was revived with a sixteen-year lease in 1907 to Horace L. Cooke, who had Mersea connections and also rented grounds at Paglesham, and the following year the manager of the Colne Fishery was reporting that Dutch buyers considered Pin Mill (Ipswich) oysters 'better fished than ours'.[14]

By 1912 three companies in the Orwell were supplying the market. The others are not named, but in 1929 appeals against rating assessments were lodged by the Roach River Co. and Smith Bros. of Burnham, which may be a clue.

Around this time Mersea smacks, including Charles Hewes's *Charlotte* and 'Dubby' French's *Waterlily*, were employed, perhaps by Horace Cooke, to work below Pin Mill, finding the tree-sheltered river such a change from the open windswept Essex estuaries that some rigged top-masts for the season there. It was remembered fondly; many years later, recalling a now closed pub, Charlie Hewes inquired 'Do the Riga still stand? I used to like Saturday nights there. Getting round the old pianner and hammering Sankey and Moody from cover to cover.' Perhaps with similar memories, Brightlingsea men would euphemistically say of a dead comrade, 'He's gone round to Pin Mill'. (Nearer home, they would also say, 'The poor old fellow's been gorn up Pyefleet these last five years'. More strangely one old deep-sea dredgerman used to refer to his voyages to the 'skilling' grounds as 'going home'.)

The Burnham companies sent their own smacks, which seem to have worked the lower grounds, as they made Trimley, not Pin Mill, their shore base. Their memories are less idyllic, for a smack's cabin did not provide luxurious accommodation for three men during the winter months which were their season there. Once a fortnight they all tried to sail home in one of the smacks, but as they had to be back for Monday morning's work, and could not wait on the weather, they had some rough passages.

There was one other curious venture in the Orwell in the 1890s. In Orwell Park Capt. Prettyman had ponds, connected by sluices with the river, in which he attempted breeding, using oyster shells fixed on wooden splines as spat collectors. According to Dr. Bulstrode he achieved some success, sending his brood after two years to other ponds at Fagborough Point, Trimley, after which it was usually sold on to other growers, only occasionally reaching the market direct. If this is true it was a remarkably early and surprisingly successful experiment in artificial hatching.

Hamford Water, today better known as Walton Backwaters, does not seem to have been much developed by its owners, the Manor of Walton. The licensing of a summer dredger in 1675 has been referred to. On that occasion another East Donyland dredgerman paid five shillings for a licence, and a St. Osyth man got one free, perhaps reflecting the fact that Lord Rochford, of St. Osyth Priory, was Lord of the Walton Manor. Around the same time there are references to a byelaw prohibiting foreigners from taking oysters, and to fines on those who did so.[15] Perhaps a further study would reveal similar regulations in earlier and later times, but on available evidence Hamford Water relapsed into common ground. The Customs officer there complained in 1775 that his boatmen passed their days 'drudging' in their seven-ton boats.[16] It may be noted that the licences in 1675 were for two dredges, whereas those at Colchester were for four, suggesting that in Hamford Water small two-man boats were used, rather than the bigger smacks of the Colne.

John Smith, of the Burnham Oyster Co., however, in 1882 obtained a Several Order covering 190 acres, arousing the usual opposition. A public meeting of objectors was held at Brightlingsea, suggesting that the Colne men dredged there, but the inquiry showed its importance was chiefly as a source of whelks. A Harwich fisherman said he had known 30 to 40 boats whelking there and Mr. Good of Harwich said his men got up to 20 wash of whelks a day, worth one to five shillings a wash. William Groom, owner of the Harwich cod smacks, declared he had known times when, if Hamford Water had not been available, fishing in the North Sea would have been stopped altogether. It was decided that Smith's order would not interfere with fishing other than oysters and mussels, but he made little use of his grant, for after a little cultivation in Hamford Water and Kirby Creek operations had ceased by 1895.[17]

Busy days at Brightlingsea

Having escaped Colchester's clutches, Brightlingsea Creek, or Borefleet as it was anciently known, seems to have been common ground, open to the people of Brightlingsea, till the beginning of the seventeenth century. Oyster layings are not mentioned in wills before this date, but such bequests are frequent thereafter.[1] If the change was made by an agreement between all the commoners it may explain the huge number of tiny patches into which Borefleet and St. Osyth Creek were divided. These layings were described as 'innumerable' in mid-nineteenth century directories, and in 1863 were estimated to number a hundred by Edward Stammers, who at the time held all the grounds in St. Osyth Creek, totalling two or three acres.[2]

How this patchwork of little plots, only about 100 feet long, were worked must remain a matter for conjecture, for native cultivation ended before living memory at Brightlingsea, and by the early 1900s the whole Creek was stocked with re-laid foreign oysters and was cleared in winter.[3] Yet throughout the nineteenth century, Brightlingsea smacks ranged far and wide, despoiling half the fisheries on the East Coast and down Channel, and must have brought home vast quantities of oysters and brood. Dredging by smacks under sail can hardly have been practicable in the Creek, and though 'haul' tow may have been employed, the phrase means nothing to the longest memories in Brightlingsea today.

It seems likelier that in the nineteenth-century heyday of the trade Brightlingsea came to prefer (or to have had the capital to afford) the quicker profits available from rapid marketing rather than the traditional husbandry still patiently practised at Mersea. Oyster merchants were given a separate classification in the mid-nineteenth century Essex directories, totalling twenty-seven in 1846 and no fewer than forty-three in 1863.

With the increasing specialisation on foreign oysters, many of the layings were acquired by London merchants, employing local managers, such as Musson & Co. and Barber & Son, who held 23 layings. The packing sheds were not adjacent to the layings, but were mostly beside the top of the Causeway, between this and James's shipyard. There were also two sheds at Underwoods Hard, above Aldous's shipyard.

According to the mid-nineteenth century directories, 'Brightlingsea Creek . . . has on either side of it innumerable oyster layings, where the fishermen lay the spat and young brood (which they gather in the Colne, Blackwater etc.) till they have grown to the size of small oysters, which then are nearly all sold to Kentish oyster merchants, who carry them to their own creeks or layings where they grow to maturity'. Another direc-tory, for 1890, states: 'A great trade is carried on at Brightlingsea in oysters, and nowhere else in the United Kingdom can such a variety and quantity be seen, as every sort in cultivation may be found here.'[4]

The varieties included Brittanies, American Bluepoints and Portuguese. In 1892 sales of 'Ports' were put at 12 million a year, and about 1,800,000 oysters were imported from America for re-laying. 'Ports' increasingly pre-dominated till, by the 1930s, most of the layings were devoted to them.

This considerable trade nearly came to an abrupt end as the result of a typhoid poisoning case around 1930, but was saved by a notable bit of co-operative enterprise. Brightlingsea Urban District Council and Tendring Rural District Council formed a Brightlingsea and Tendring Shellfish Com-mittee, and a cleansing plant was set up around 1933 on the site of the present Brightlingsea Sailing Club under the direction of the Ministry of Agriculture and Fisheries Experimental Station at Conway.

The cleansing process was long and laborious. The merchants brought their oysters to the plant, having to wash their boots in a chlorine bath before entering. The oysters were then spread thinly, about two layers deep, on wooden grids and hosed with sterile sea-water to remove mud and dirt from the shells, using a specially designed hose-rake. After this

A Brightlingsea smack in Pyefleet Creek, c.1905.

water had been flushed away, the tank was filled for twenty-four hours with sterile water, which remained perfectly clear so long as the oysters were all healthy. The next day the water was run off and the oysters, after being again hosed down, were given another bath for up to twenty hours, again watching for any dirtying of the water, a sign that a moribund oyster was failing to cleanse itself. The process was repeated yet again on the third day, with the oysters covered for one hour with sterile water containing two parts per million of chlorine. The purpose of this was to sterilise the shells and the grids on which they lay. The oysters would not open in chlorinated water, so there was no question of their flavour being affected.

The sterile water for the first and second baths was obtained by adding chlorine solution to the extent of three parts per million. After standing for at least twelve hours the chlorine was neutralised by the addition of 'hypo' (sodium thiosulphate). The water for the first and second baths also had to be pre-heated by boilers to a temperature between 54 and 58 degrees Fahrenheit.

The station had seven tanks, some covered, some out-of-doors for summer use, in which the merchants' consignments were kept apart by laying partitions of non-porous bricks. Throughput in the first year amounted to two million, rising to a peak of four million in 1938 and 1939. The trade collapsed with the outbreak of war, and afterwards never fully recovered. The charge for cleansing was sixpence per hundred, ultimately rising to 1s. 6d. No Brightlingsea natives were put through, but occasionally a local merchant cleansed a consignment of Truro natives, presumably to secure the Association's seal and guarantee of purity. All consignments had of course to go direct from the station to the purchaser, and for this purpose the merchants were allowed to store them for up to ten days in the tanks. Some 'Ports' were opened on the premises, and the meat packed in sterilised tins or cartons. Every basket or bag was also sterilised before being sealed.

The plant operated till the 1962/3 winter ended cultivation in Brightlingsea. Throughout the whole of its existence its Superintendent, Burgess Everett, was proud to recall that he had only one complaint, which was traced to the folly of a customer who thought a dirty ditch would be a good place to store his order.[5]

In addition to the great trade in every kind of re-laid oyster, and to the Colchester Oyster Fishery of which it was effectively the headquarters, Brightlingsea was the chief Essex centre for yet another oyster fishery, the deep-sea dredging described in the following chapters, and was busily employed on oyster smack building. The heyday of its bustling enterprise, the last quarter of the nineteenth century, was affectionately recorded by its Rector, Canon Arthur Pertwee, who cared for and understood his maritime flock, for he often went on North Sea dredging voyages and recorded his interests and experiences in his monthly notes in his parish magazine.

New oyster grounds were still being discovered and smacks built, bought or lengthened to dredge them. New wholesale markets for deep-sea oysters were opened up at Southend and Ipswich. In 1882 the fleet fitting out for Jersey, Swansea, Caernarvon and Grimsby was increased by smacks acquired from Ramsgate, Dover, Beaumaris, Jersey and Grimsby, in addition to new tonnage continually being built at the three local yards, which in 1885 launched no fewer than eighteen oyster boats, large and small, many of them for Mersea and Tollesbury, where the outlook for the domestic fisheries was equally optimistic.[6] The little town held its own oyster feast at the Swan Hotel in 1882 (claiming to revive an old custom) and the following year followed this with a Young Mariners Tea Party, when one of the songs sung was 'The Fisherboys of Hull'. This, said the Vicar, 'might serve to remind the apprentice lads of Brightlingsea of the difference between their condition and some in other places. Instead of being treated like slaves they had as a rule a kind master and a good home'. This will doubtless bring a cynical smile to the lips of today's sociologists, ever picking through the past in the hope of identifying worker-oppression and social protest. But it is well founded, since Brightlingsea, as well as being one of the last fishing ports to keep up the apprentice tradition, also never departed from personal skipper-ownership. It was the commercially managed fleets of Grimsby and Hull that victimised their apprentices so brutally. In 1891 there were sixty-three apprentices to sea fishing in the port of Colchester (only four other places had more), and in the four preceding years not one had gone to prison. Harwich then had only 24 and had seen one go to prison.

A skiff full of slipper limpets, a pest of American origin, dredged on the Colne fishery and ready for dumping ashore.

Before long, however, some ominous shadows fell across this sunny prospect. A disaster to the deep-sea 'skilling' fleet, described in the next chapter, was too much even for a community accustomed to a continual loss of life among its mariners. The deep-sea oysters themselves, large, coarse and popular for selling on fairgrounds and at race meetings, also lost their place in a market now catering for the gentry. Brightlingsea was also among the places involved in the pollution problems of the 1890s, already mentioned, which must have affected markets and may have contributed to the abandonment of native cultivation. The big smacks increasingly turned to scallop dredging, and a few unsuccessfully tried cod lining. Others were sold back to the ports from which they had been obtained. Unhappily the other Brightlingsea staple, spratting, was also in decline, pending the introduction of canning which brought a revival just before the First World War.

In 1901, when six vessels were sold away, the old Canon was regretting 'the gradual decline of the fishing fleet, which threatens to become extinct', and six years later he was noting that the young men were 'scattered over the high seas – 20 to 30 in the River Plate, others in the Cape and Australia liners'. Still, he reflected, this was 'better than standing about at home'.

The Skillingers

The longest voyages undertaken by the Essex smacks were not in fact in search of deep-sea oysters, but to the Forth on the East Coast and the Solway on the West. These odysseys – to challenge the fishermen from the little Scottish port of Newhaven on the grounds of Edinburgh Corporation and the Duke of Buccleugh, and to garner the riches of Luce Bay – were in search of brood stocks of the flat native oysters once common in most of the estuaries and on the offshore shoals and sandbanks around the British Isles and along much of the continental coast from Denmark to Brittany.

Thus not only the big deep-sea smacks made long voyages; even little twelve-tonners such as the Mersea *Snowdrop* would leave their familiar creeks for a summer cruise as far as Falmouth, and others no bigger would try their luck down Channel or off the Norfolk coast. These visits to distant places were, in effect, an extension of the domestic cultivation, necessary because the Essex fisheries, from the earliest stages of their development, were never self-supporting through their own spatfalls, but required massive and regular transfusions of stock from elsewhere – a fact to be borne in mind in considering their ultimate long terminal decline. An oyster dredgermen's petition in 1736 said that Essex dredgers went to the western channel to take brood to fatten on their layings. The Customs said the oysters were imported only into Rochester, Faversham, Colchester and Maldon, amounting to 213,897 bushels between 1718 and 1735.[1] This was not a one-way trade, for the Jersey and French cultivators also bought brood from the Blackwater to lay on their own beds.[2]

The real deep-sea trade was quite different, and it is not always easy to know where to draw the line or, more accurately, to decide on which side of the line some of the 'foreign' ventures should be placed, though there is sometimes a clue from the fact that deep-sea oysters were reckoned by the thousand and inshores by the bushel or wash.

The deep-sea oyster, found off Friesland and along the French coast between Dunkirk and Cherbourg in water up to twenty-four fathoms deep, was large, deep-shelled and coarse-flavoured. It was worked by big sea-going smacks which were the crowning glory of all Essex working sail, using huge dredges with hoeing edges up to six feet wide. These could not be hand-hauled like the inshore dredges, but were cranked in using hand-winches or 'winks' on three-inch bass warps. Up to six dredges would be used, through fairleads and rollers on the rail or a port in the bulwarks. The smacks lay to, often with topmasts struck, under reefed mainsail or trysail, hauling day and night, for the working day began at six a.m. and continued till three a.m. – often for a week on end. By 1874 Colchester had a fleet of 132 of these 'first class' smacks of fifteen to fifty tons, mostly owned at Brightlingsea, with twenty-nine at Rowhedge and about a dozen each at Wivenhoe and Tollesbury. Few were owned at West Mersea (though the *Mayflower* was lost off the Isle of Wight in 1831 and the *Nancy* off Jersey in 1845), but Burnham had its own fleet, working largely down to the Channel Islands.[3]

The best remembered of the true deep-sea fisheries was that of Terschelling, about 112 miles north-east of Orford Ness, from which point the smacks usually took their departure. It was not the most ancient, for it only came into prominence around 1877, but in the thirty years it lasted it took an unprecedented toll of life and limb – the reason why its memory is so deeply etched in local memory – because the grounds lay on what was usually a lee shore, open to the full savagery of the North Sea, with no harbour of refuge available during the two-week voyages.

These were the conditions encountered by a fleet of eight Brightlingsea 'skillingers' (as they came to be called) in March 1883. One Thursday evening the *Express* returned with a flag in her rigging for a lost member of her crew, followed by the damaged *Glance, Vanduara, Drean, Care* and *Heiress.* Three others never returned. The surviving skippers gathered on the Hard, 'walking an imaginary deck's length' in cutting snow squalls, speculating as to their fate. The *Recruit* had been seen by the *Gemini* on the previous Tuesday, with her boom broken; her crew 'wove' and saluted. The lugger *Mascotte* was thought to have been lost on Haisboro Sands. (She was probably an ex-lugger converted to smack rig.) The *Conquest,* it was conjectured, was lost on the Dutch coast. One of her crew, twenty-three years old Charles Barber, had been rescued only the previous month when the smack *Diligent* was dismasted.

The following January two more smacks, *Pride* and *William and Henry* also disappeared without trace in the North Sea. Canon Pertwee observed: 'Surely the sad and stern logic of facts has proved the folly of venturing to the Terschelling grounds during the winter months. During the past year five smacks have been lost in the North Sea. In that vast cemetery we have buried twice as many men as in the old churchyard at home.'[4] It was, he declared, 'an unequal struggle, which bravely as it has been maintained by the mariners of Brightlingsea, it were madness to prolong.' The following July, however, the canon was not afraid to go on a 'skilling' voyage in the *Christabel,* which he described as an ex-pilot cutter. He revelled in it, boasting that they did the first 170 miles in eighteen and a half hours, and 'when coming up the Wellet (*sic*) in her holiday clothes she was mistaken by some observers for the celebrated yacht *Lorna*'. Two years later he made another voyage in Charles Brasted's *Palace,* conducting a service that included 'The Skilling Tune' (which alas he fails to identify).

The stern warnings were not heeded, though some of the smacks turned to coasting, scalloping and other occupations. In 1884 *Excellent* and *White Rose* both did well, but in bad weather had to lay to for eight and eleven days respectively. The canon and his curate rowed off to welcome them home. The newly-built *Majestic* by contrast suffered from summer heat and calms, only getting 3,350 oysters for seventy-eight hours' work, and most of these died on the way home. To avoid this sort of problem several smacks were being fitted with wells, and one of these, *Care*, a survivor of the 1883 disaster, was also lengthened and renamed *Lady Olive*. In May 1885 she was rewarded with the record catch of 40,000 oysters, though in September Canon Pertwee confusingly reports that '*Lady Olive*, which usually holds 15,000, has this trip only taken 12,000, as the oysters are so large'.

In the autumn of that year the *Leith*, a former Harwich cod smack and the largest of the fleet, was blown on to the coast of Jutland, where she found good oysters, bringing home 31,000. The *Four Brothers* started home in a south-westerly gale in December, but suffered damage and had to bear away for Heligoland. Entering the Elbe she brought up at Cuxhaven, and was towed to Hamburg, where she sold her oysters. Leaving the Elbe on December 17 she got in two more days' work, reached Lowestoft on Christmas Day and was home the same evening. Truly, if a Brightlingsea man of that age had found himself crossing the Styx, he would have compelled Charon to heave-to the ferry to let him chuck a dredge over – and would have found a buyer for his catch in Hell!

Not all the disasters were in the North Sea. In October 1884 Charles Barber (father of the lad lost in the *Conquest*) made a voyage to Whitstable with brood with his two other sons. They started back only to disappear. Ultimately the Whitstable divers found the wreck near the Ridge Buoy in the Whitaker Channel with damage showing she had been run down. Barber's son-in-law, Oscar Salmon, had also been lost in the *Mascotte*, of which he was skipper. So Mrs. Barber had lost a husband, three sons and a son-in-law – and was to lose another son-in-law, John Ellis, from the Newhaven smack, *Ripple*, four years later.

Reverting to the 'skilling' story, the *Vanduara* and *Lady Olive* both came home in November 1885 with broken gaffs, and the *Matchless* with her bulwarks gone. The following January the *Heiress* reported she had made five trips since being lengthened and welled at Wivenhoe shipyard, averaging 31,030 oysters a trip – a record. Her skipper, William King (who was perhaps partial to seeing his name in the Parish Magazine) was claiming another record in March 1886 with a catch of 42,000, though the market was now in decline and they were worth only the value of 30,000 three years previously. But it was a long trip, taking twenty days. The *Gipsy Queen* was also away for eighteen days, the passage home taking a week. Both smacks must have been glad of their wells.

Ten other smacks also turned to 'skilling' that spring, with the end of the stowboat season, while ten others preferred scalloping. Later that year the *Heiress* broke her own record with a catch of 44,800 on an eighteen-day voyage, and also managed 24,000 in three days.

The *Heiress*'s record was broken in 1887 by the *Guide*, which took 49,000 oysters in nineteen days, but in the same year the sale of deep-sea oysters was banned by the Corporation of the City of London between June 15 and August 7. The loss of the summer season, on top of the poor prices, was a major setback. Brightlingsea protested that the ban should affect only English oysters whereas 'skillingers' were 'Dutch and no more English than if they were Australian or Chinese'. Yet still some smacks stuck to the trade. The *Excellent* rescued the crew of a Delfzyl timber schooner thirty miles north east of Texel on her last trip in 1887, skipper Wheeler being presented with a barometer by the Shipwrecked Fishermen's and Mariners' Society. The *Leith* was fitted with steam power for her dredges in 1890 by her Brightlingsea owner, John Sawyer, who also bought the fifty-eight ton *Hawthorn* from Harwich. The two were put back experimentally in their old codfishing trade in the Orkneys and Faroes, but without success, due to 'weather, lack of experience and lack of hands'.

Yet another disaster occurred in 1891 with the loss of the *Glance*, which sailed on January 10. She was not expected home till the first week in February, and there was no great anxiety even when the *Hilda*, returning with bulwarks damaged in a gale, reported she had seen the *Glance* hove-to on January 14. Then the *Heiress* put in to report that forty miles off Borkum she had run across a waterlogged boat with the *Glance's* name on it, torn from its lashings and with the stem ripped out. Not till Sunday 15 February, were the blinds drawn and the flags half-masted at Brightlingsea, as it was accepted that the *Glance* had probably gone down in the same storm which damaged the *Hilda*. The Canon, preaching to a crowded church from the text, 'I know not the day of my death', observed that in his eighteen years at Brightlingsea he had seen 101 lives lost at sea. He re-opened the shipwreck disaster fund he had started in March 1883, and soon needed to call on it for a disaster to the Channel fleet recounted in the next chapter.

The big smacks were now being sold off, *Emblem* and *Thought* to Iceland, where they were delivered by Brightlingsea crews, and *Gipsy Queen* to Emsworth. Brightlingsea men joined the exodus to Grimsby, which also sent smacks to the 'skilling', including *Orcadian* (built at Brightlingsea as well as crewed by Brightlingsea men) and *Jenny*. Between 1889 and 1896 seven former Brightlingsea men were lost in the Grimsby *Oyster Girl, Jimmy Campbell, Perseverence* and *Sobriety*. At home the survivors reported little oddities to relieve the continual chronicle of men lost overboard and failing markets. *Matchless* had her masthead on fire, presumably from lightning, with damage to topmast and topsail. *Countess* kept her topsail set for three weeks in the North Sea. But mostly it was a continuation of the old grim story. *Jenny C, Hawthorn* and *Excellent* all came in damaged in 1895, when Sawyer's *Olive* (another former Harwich cod smack) taking North Sea oysters to Frederickshaven in Denmark was wrecked off Jutland. On a calm night she anchored with eighty fathoms of kedge rope which broke as they tried to get under way. Her crew was saved, but the oysters had to be given away at 1s. 8d. a hundred.

As the new century opened *Majestic* and *Countess* were sold away and *Prima Donna*, recently bought from Grimsby, returned to her previous owners there. *Emma* sailed to the 'skilling' grounds in January 1901 but returned with so much damage to her bulwarks and timber-heads that she could not work her dredges. By 1903 the *Bee,* a Rye-built ketch by this time owned at Grimsby, was the only vessel going to the old grounds. She came back with a broken bowsprit and other damage, having been swept by big seas. An injured member of her crew was brought ashore up the Hard in a cart, as so many of his mates had been before him. Thus ended the hardest and cruellest trade Essex men ever took part in.

Down channel dredgers

The other chief deep-sea fisheries were down Channel. They were of greater importance and longer duration than the 'skilling', and less hazardous because of the availability of harbours of refuge, though those on the French shore were liable to offer a hostile reception.

Off Jersey rich beds were discovered in 1797, though their rights were disputed up to 1822, when a settlement was reached.[1] Soon the new grounds were attracting a fleet of 300 smacks from Essex, Shoreham, Emsworth and Faversham, manned by 2,000 dredgermen and converting the little port of Gorey into a boom town. This was not the start of the long link between Essex and the Channel Islands, for Alston's of Leigh observed in 1820 that there had been no great importation since 1792, but now with the French Wars over they wanted better facilities from the Customs.[2] By this time (1820) fifty-nine smacks registered in the port of Maldon (which then included Burnham and Tollesbury) were working in the winter to Jersey, making up to eight voyages in a year, though most made only one or two. In 1823 over 84,000 bushels were imported in seventy voyages. A dozen smacks brought Jersey oysters into Leigh in 1843, and in 1846 importing was extended to the Blackwater by the Tollesbury Oyster Co., so some at least of these cargoes were probably brood rather than deep-sea oysters.

The Jersey trade was carried on throughout the Napoleonic Wars, but with the end of hostilities friction with the French became acute as the English dredgers were attracted to the rich beds along the French mainland. In 1832 the Colne fleet returned home complaining of lack of Naval protection, and the following year the *Hebe* of Brightlingsea was seized by a French gunboat and her crew set adrift, alleging that a British gunboat *Seaflower* made no attempt to intercede.

Prompted by such incidents as this, the House of Commons in 1833 set up a Select Committee to inquire into the British Channel Fisheries, which recommended a close season from 1 May to 31 August and a limit of two and a half inches for oysters taken. No legislation seems to have followed, but in 1839 a Convention was agreed with the French government which not only accepted the close season but made any dredge liable to seizure. This showed an abysmal ignorance of oyster cultivation, as it prohibited moving of stock and the clearing of grounds during the summer months, yet it duly became law in 1844. Fortunately no officer of the Customs, Coastguard or Navy seems to have availed himself of the powers given to him to seize the first dredge he saw. In fact the legislation was largely ignored, till in 1852 on the insistence of the French the close season was generally enforced down Channel and in the Channel Islands (including the inshore fisheries within the three mile limit) though no attempt was made to stop summer dredging in Essex and Kent. Ultimately, in 1875, the Board of Trade ruled that it should not be applied anywhere within the three-mile limit. (A close season for dredging, intended to conserve stocks, should not be confused with the traditional avoidance of oysters 'when there is not an R in the month', and they are unfit for consumption because they are spatting.) In 1889 the French government abandoned the close season for oysters above 5cm, but three years later a meeting of oyster planters at Billingsgate decided to exclude them from sale in the same way as English ones. 'Channels' now seem to have been quite out of favour; Canon Pertwee lamented in that year, 'if the price of deep-seas were only a quarter the price of natives!' New grounds were found at Etaples ('Eat Apple Bay' to the Brightlingsea men), in 1904, but too late to be of value.

The French grounds became increasingly important as the Jersey fishery began to fail in 1845, and despite some attempts at re-stocking and the discovery in 1849 of a new ground, forty miles long, between Guernsey and Jersey, they were finally exhausted by 1871.

The Convention did little to relieve the strain of international relations. In 1838 the *Gazette Dieppois* was complaining that 'fifteen or sixteen English fishing boats from Colchester have entered our port for the purpose of fishing oysters at Cap D'Ailly. Our authorities do nothing to keep them away', and two years later the Consul warned Brightlingsea men to stay away from Dieppe. In 1885 the Brightlingsea boats were fitting out for Caen Bay, but two years later some preferred to dredge off Ostend 'where they were not molested ashore'.[3]

At other times, however, the Essex men seem to have been accepted. In 1883 the English Sailors' Reading Rooms and Seamen's Home were well used at Le Havre, where the Brightlingsea crews were visited by Rev. G.C.L. Hall and his father, Rev. E. Hall, Rector of Myland, who preached at a service aboard the smack *Rosa Ann*. Only two years after this, however, there was trouble when seven Brightlingsea smacks (*Honour, Velocity, Union, Ripple, Rosa Ann, Billow* and *Welcome*) along with one from Tollesbury and one from Caernarvon, were detained. They sailed in and then found the lock gate closed to prevent them leaving, the pretext being that under the Convention they were only allowed in in bad weather. They were finally released after intervention by James Round, M.P. Yet in 1896 it was reported that 'the Reading Rooms at Le Havre are again pleasantly used'.

Soon after the incident of 1885 two carriers from Southwick, near Southampton, were boarded by Mr. Crush, the Burnham merchant, who testified that 'not over five per cent of the oysters were under size' – a discovery with which a modern fisheries inspector might have been less easily satisfied.[4] The Brightlingsea smacks, however, were apparently able to keep their big catches of up to 30,000 oysters alive in their wet wells, which were now regarded as essential, without relying on sending a carrier home during the voyage, though an occasional cargo perished when they were becalmed.

The Channel dredgers did not suffer as many disasters, or so severe a toll of life, as the 'skillingers', because of the availability of harbours of refuge. They were, however, often swept by the long Channel seas, to which their low freeboard and flush decks made them vulnerable. *Norman* returned from Caen in 1897 with damage to her sails and boat, and Bowles' fine ketch *First* was run down and sunk there in the same year by a Portsmouth smack. She was carrying money for Bowles' other smack *Countess*.

A November gale in 1891 brought the worst disaster down Channel. The *Volunteer, Sisters, Gemini* and *Test* were working in Caen Bay and thinking of returning home for the stowboat season. They came out of Le Havre on a Tuesday morning, intending another day's work, but as the wind was fair they showed flares as they had agreed and set out. *Volunteer* reached Brightlingsea on the Thursday morning with damaged rails and bulwarks and a smashed boat. Then at midday came a telegram from Ramsgate reporting that *Gemini* had been towed in with the loss of four of her crew of six, including her skipper, John Causton, whose son was one of the two survivors. All had been swept overboard off Dover. The skipper's last words were 'God's will be done'.

The *Test* arrived in the evening, with only three men aboard, all injured. Her skipper, John French, and one hand had been swept overboard off the *Royal Sovereign*. The survivors reported she had hove-to from midnight till six a.m. on Wednesday, then made sail till ten and hove-to again. At midday they had sighted breakers ahead. The *Test* would not bear away, and the sea filled the cabin. William Gould's leg was jammed between the boat and the boom jaws. The skipper's farewell was, 'We are all lost, brothers. Lord have mercy upon me and upon my poor Bob.' The injured survivors put the chain round the flukes of the anchor and let go forty fathoms, along with the kedge. They then drove till they saw the lights of Calais, where they brought up, rigged the smack despite a broken gaff, and sailed her home. The *Sisters* ultimately arrived safely, with one man injured, having been helped into Ramsgate.

By the turn of the century, the fleet was being sold off and men were finding other occupations. In October 1897 the smacks were unusually late off to Caen due to difficulty in getting crews till more yachts came home. Yet as late as 1904 *Excellent, Rapid, Olive* and *Norma*, 'the best fishing vessels of their class for dredging work', were re-surveyed by the Board of Trade for 'Caen and Eat Apple Bay', and were altered at Aldeburgh, having their focs'les extended for stowing sails. (For stowboating by contrast the cabin was often reduced to provide space to carry a few more tons of sprats.) This enterprise was ill-rewarded, for sailing craft now faced a new hazard dreaded as much as wind and weather – the carelessly navigated steamship. *Norma* was run down in the same year by a mail steamer off Boulogne and heavily damaged, while *Lady Olive,* working ten miles off Dunkirk with 10,000 oysters aboard, was hit by the collier *Narcissus.* Her crew scrambled aboard the collier as she sank in eighteen fathoms in six minutes, all lights burning.

Excellent, leaving Dunkirk, hit the pier and sank, but was towed home for repairs by Aldous. In 1908 she was the only smack oyster-dredging from Dunkirk, and in 1912 she returned with 'a good catch of oysters and scallops, taken in thick fog off the French coast, so her skipper, Gunn, did not know where'.[5]

The Essex dredgermen made both enemies and friends on their long voyages. In the Firth of Forth they needed police protection and slept in Newhaven Harbour with a poker and hatchet handy beside the bunk. Their annual arrival at Falmouth was awaited with apprehension. [6]

Elsewhere relations were more cordial. The rich Swansea grounds were dredged out to re-stock Essex and Kentish beds by a fleet of smacks up to 200 strong, provoking the Mayor of Swansea to voice the usual ineffective call for conservation and control as long ago as 1844. Yet the fishermen of Mumbles were so impressed by the Essex smacks that about 1855 a delegation travelled to Colneside, leading to several orders for twelve-tonners to be built in local yards. Later these were copied by a Bristol Channel builder, and were in turn imitated for a small class of Brixham cutters, known as 'Mumble Bees'. Mumbles in 1873 employed 200 boats and sold nine million oysters – three times the total achieved by the Colne in number, though probably not in value. The Swansea fishery was, however, by this time in severe decline – blamed on the inertia of the Corporation and the use of an undersize two-inch ring – and became extinct just after the First World War.[7]

Several Colne men chose to settle in remote Whithorn[8] and an ex-Brightlingsea man, William Brasted, was lost in a Whitehaven trawler in 1883. Probably many more such settlers could be found, but nowhere (except perhaps for the general exodus to Grimsby at the end of the century) in greater number than at Emsworth, where the broad vowels of Brightlingsea became as familiar as the softer Sussex speech.

Like most of its neighbours on the Sussex coast, including Newhaven, Shoreham and Bosham, Emsworth had a substantial and ancient fishery, and as early as 1814 Colne smacks were denuding the harbour of spat.[9] Then in 1875 an innovator remarkable even by the standards of his age, John Duncan Foster, started his own oyster and scallop business, building first fifty-foot cutters, then sixty-five-foot ketches and finally a series of big ketches unparalleled in this country, with the profile of the contemporary racing yachts, including schooner bow and cutaway forefoot, with steam capstans for their dredges. The culmination was the 110-foot ketch *Echo,* probably the most extreme fishing vessel in Britain, with an auxiliary steam engine working a propeller as well as five steam capstans. She was launched in 1903, on the eve of the poisoning disaster already mentioned, which dealt a disastrous blow to Foster's business and his prestige, for after being awarded £3,300 damages against Warblington Council (he estimated his total losses at over £80,000) he lost his claim on appeal, and was hooted through the streets by the ratepayers. Despite these misfortunes and the closure of harbour layings and pits till a new sewerage scheme was completed in 1914, this extraordinary man went on to build a larger and improved *Echo*, which was being fitted out when war started in 1914, and for that reason was never completed.[10]

This remarkable fleet worked alongside the Essex-men on the Channel oyster and scallop grounds which were continually being discovered off the Sussex coast, and was largely crewed by Brightlingsea men, for it was reaching its peak at the time Brightlingsea was losing heart, just as twenty years before Brightlingsea had taken over some of the last of the obsolete Harwich codlining smacks, though in this case few if any Harwich men came with them.

When the *Thistle* of Emsworth was lost off Beachy Head in 1889 several members of her crew were Brightlingsea men who had settled there, and the following year a young Brightlingsea man, Albert Rouse, son of the skipper, was lost overboard from the *Sybil*. The interchange was mutual, for in the same year an Emsworth man was lost from the Brightlingsea *Gipsy Queen*, which as already mentioned was herself sold to Emsworth in 1894.

The smacks used each other's ports freely. The *Leith* put into Emsworth with a huge cargo of 60,000 oysters in 1890, and the same year *Sybil* arrived at Brightlingsea to sign on a crew. Foster's *Ostrea* was returning to Brightlingsea from the 'skilling' in 1892 with a Brightlingsea crew when she got ashore on the Gunfleet. As she was loaded with 32,000 oysters her crew gave her up for lost and took to their boat. After two hours' rowing in the dark they saw a vessel lying to nearby and found it to be the *Ostrea* which had floated off undamaged.

Emsworth kept up the traditional deep-sea dredging into the 1930s and has seen a revival with the transfer of the Several Order to the Fishermen's Federation Ltd. in 1974. It thus outlived Brightlingsea, as well as surpassing it in the final flowering of the trade. The partnership makes an interesting page in the history of both places.

Flags, fists and firearms

The placid and harmless oyster has down the centuries shown a remarkable capacity for provoking dispute, dishonesty, litigation and violence.

As long ago as the reign of Edward III, during the disputes with Lionel de Bradenham, a fracas among the men of Brightlingsea, Alresford, Wivenhoe, Fingringhoe, Mersea, Salcott and Tollesbury over fishing rights in the Geedon Creek and 'Parrock Flete' (often referred to, and perhaps the old name of Pyefleet) ended in the drowning of three men[1], and from that time onward layings have been plundered, not only by strangers but often by the men who collectively owned them. Ownership itself has been challenged through innumerable, angry and expensive resorts to law, some of which have already been mentioned, and even by openly provocative displays of force, some of which it is now time to describe.

Before doing so, it is worth considering some of the circumstances which compelled oyster fisheries to set up not only protection associations, but, in the case of the larger concerns, private police forces – something unparalleled in other forms of husbandry and industry.

It has to be remembered that, while the small layings in the creeks were well marked by withies and notices which clearly proclaimed them as private estates, other grounds were usually the bed of navigable estuaries which before the time of turnpike roads and railways were the chief highways for trade and commerce of all kinds. The sub-marine riches were invisible, their territory marked on maps and perhaps by a few 'metes' ashore, but undiscernible to the eye. Thus a few years' neglect could dispel any memories of private ownership, leading to a belief that they were common property, founded no doubt at first on wishful opportunism, but often developing into a general popular conviction. In the course of these researches, a Maldon old-timer observed: 'I believe some fellow from Burnham once tried to tell us we couldn't dredge in Walton backwaters. I'd like to know what he thought he was up to.'

Legal rights, at best hardly comprehensible to trained minds and quite beyond the understanding of simple dredgermen, were confused by the way monarchs bestowed and manors laid claim to titles already established, and the way corporate boroughs allowed their charters to be suspended, leading to periods of doubt and confusion. 'Prescriptive' rights were often interpreted as 'exclusive' – a fruitful cause of controversy. Even when such rights were not in dispute, the law was eccentric in defending them. Oyster pillaging was so severe along the south coast in the early nineteenth century that a Select Committee of the House of Commons was set up in 1833, yet in 1814 a Colchester dredgerman named Richardson, convicted of taking three gallons of spat from Chichester Harbour for his private layings, successfully appealed to the Queen's Bench on the grounds that the law referred to the destruction of fish, and his object was to preserve them!

This circumstantial background may to some extent explain the extraordinary outbreaks of feuding and fisticuffs which were such a feature of the oyster world, conducted as they were not clandestinely but with the maximum parade of publicity and self justifying bravado.

The first such raid of which detailed records exist came in 1725 when a hundred smacks manned by 500 men of Queenborough and Faversham 'invaded the Hadleigh Ray with flags flying and the firing of guns', and also stripped the grounds newly established off Southend by Outing. According to John Lee, whose account of Outing's pioneering venture has already been quoted:

'They came in a body, of about five hundred with six Sloops besides small craft. Being far too great a body for them to oppose, they apply'd to two or three Justices of the Peace who ordered the two High Constables to summon the Petty Constables of Rotchford hundred to attend them, and the Justices next day went upon the Shore . . . the Kentish men being there, gathering oysters, Captain Evans, who was then Mayor of Qeenbourrough, and also their Member of Parliament, and also one Gabriel Ruck of Milton, a rich dredger, where the Riot Act was read, and so within the hour they all got on board their vessels, pulled off their hats, gave a loud shout, King George for ever, and went home that day so no Violence was attempted, [but] toock afterwards as many as they pleased, and where they pleased . . . The Captain, and Mr. Ruck, desired them to give way in a very civil manner. They also cleared Hadleigh Ray, above Leigh.

'Mr. Outing brought an Action of trespas for so many acres as they had robbed against Captain Evans, and Mr. Ruck; so did Mr. Hutton, Sir Francis Saint John's tennant, for Hadleigh Ray, being a large place; and Daniel Scratton's tennants did the same. Chelmsford people having affronted Lord Chief Justice Pratt, by refusing to pay the Inn keeper at the Bell for their keeping, he stopped them; for which reason the next year, 1725, the Assizes were at Brentwood, and only that year; where Hutton and Outing's causes were tryed, and Hutton had two Thousand pound dammage allowed him and cost of suit besides; and Mr. Outing had one thousand one hundred pound dammage given him, and also charges . . .

'And the other, Mr. Scratton's tenant for Prittlewell shore, they chose to be tryed . . . at Westminster Hall, by a special jury view of Gentlemen, Sir Robert Abdy, Bart, being foreman; before three Judges who came into Court about tenn Clock in the forenoon, there being no less than six Councill of a side, all Serjeants at large; there being also about Sixty Witnesses; the Judges did not go out of Court nor stir, and where, till after three a'Clock next morning, that a Verdict was brought in, having Wine and Biscuits brought them; but the Councill, the Jury and the rest, the Judges allowed them by their Watches exactly an hour and no more . . . Just as the clocks struck three, two thousand one hundred pound Damage was declared, with cost, which was of course a great deal. I was told the Essex Council had 20 guineas a piece, and Serjeant Pingelley, as Senior, 25 guineas, and the Jurie well paid, and Elegantly treated, all the Witnesses too, who went with Musick and Cockades in their hats, Shouting and singing, at four in the Morning, through the City, to White Chappel, people riseing to their windows to see what it was.

'The Kentish gentlemen paid in near Seven Thousand pounds, if not more, being greatly mistaken about it being common, for the Lords of the Manors produced grants from the Crown, to low water mark, which were read in Court, the Oysters lying a long way above that. It is certain they had a great many, for . . . they loaded five large Sloops, carrying them all directly, and so fast to London made a glut at market'.

Lee adds that it took Milton, Queenborough and Faversham many years to pay off the damages and costs awarded, 'Faversham above twenty, was said'.

This is one of the few occasions when Essex men were the innocent party. More often they were themselves the aggressors, though it may be noted that they made no comparable raids on Kentish fisheries, perhaps because these were too firmly established in the general consciousness to admit of the doubts and suspicions which afforded the pretext for militancy in the way already described.[2] Orford, in Suffolk, was another matter. Here a Corporation fishery was based on grants by Edward VI and Elizabeth I. Like Harwich it was raided by fleets of Colne smacks, certainly as long ago as 1770. After Orford Corporation had refused an application by the 'Mayor of Brightlingsea'[3] to lease the fishery, matters came to a head with the disastrous winter of 1788 which wiped out the stocks of all the Essex fisheries. Colne and Burnham boats were tempted into the Orford river, which being deeper seems to have survived better.

Ten smacks from Brightlingsea were warned away in August 1790, but a fortnight later four more, including two of the previous fleet, were caught dredging in the night. They were taken to Orford Quay, where it was found that each had over 30 bushels of oysters and brood. The masters were taken before Samuel Randall, J.P., the Earl of Hertford and other members of the Corporation, and after being reprimanded and threatened with prosecution, promised not to come into Orford again 'unless by stress of weather'.

The following January, however, twelve more smacks arrived and were opposed by the Orford boats. In a strong north-west wind Mark Noble's *Mary Ann* ran down an Orford boat off the lower end of Havergate Island, sinking her, after which the invaders put to sea. Then on 9 February, twenty-six smacks came in, followed the next day by twenty-six more. The whole fleet of fifty-two smacks, of ten to thirty tons, including Noble's *Mary Ann*, dredged till they were full and sailed away.

On 12 February, twelve more appeared, dredging right up to the town, but the Orford men successfully seized their catch and thirty-six dredges. When three more arrived on 4 March their masters were committed to gaol and after five or six days they were released on recognisances to attend at the next Sessions. Finally a fleet of twenty-four smacks arrived, one flying a Commodore's flag and bearing an employee of a Colchester attorney, Mr. Smythies, who was also Town Clerk.

The hearings were at Bury Assizes in August 1791, the defendants being John Richardson and William Winterflood, John Tabor, 'Mayor' of Brightlingsea and owner of several smacks, and Matthew Tabor, master of the smack *Liberty*. The defence claimed that Orford had lost its charter, leaving the river a free fishery, but the verdict upheld the town's 'sole and exclusive rights'.[4]

Militant disputes now began to centre on Burnham, suggesting that century-old grievances over the Crouch smouldered on, and perhaps more immediately as a response to the company formed in 1780, which no doubt set up its own defences against casual poaching.

Dame Anne Mildmay complained in 1789 that 'disorderly persons had threatened to enter the fishery and dredge for oysters', and in 1808 Hawkins & Co. noted that 'an unlawful conspiracy had been entered into by several oyster merchants in and near Brightlingsea for the purpose of coming into the fishery in a large body and by force dredging for oysters there'.[5]

This threat had already been carried into action in March 1807 when thirty or forty smacks from Wivenhoe and Rowhedge sailed into the Crouch and started to dredge in response to a signal from one of them flying a flag at her masthead. The Burnham Customs tide surveyor, Charles Bull, went off with a constable and boarded the *Betsey* of Rowhedge, taking off the Master, J. Willett and two hands. The Colne men assembled aboard one of the other smacks, planning to rescue the prisoners, who were, however, taken before two magistrates and committed to jail for felony.

The following January oysters valued at hundreds of pounds were carried off, and later in the same month, despite an injunction secured by the Burnham merchants, a fleet of thirty-five smacks from 'Brightlingsea and other ports of the Colne' arrived 'for the purpose of stripping the oyster layings of Sir Henry Mildmay, Bart.'. Captain Rutherford of the Sea Fencibles 'exhorted them to desist', but the raiders were not deterred by him or even by the appearance among them of a boat containing three ecclesiastical J.P.s, The Rev. H. B. Dudley (Bradwell's noted sporting parson), Rev. M. Wise and Rev. Dr. Scott.

CAUTION

TO

OYSTER DREDGERS.

WHEREAS Information having been received by Messrs. Hawkins and Co. of Burnham, Oyster Dredgers, who occupy under Sir Henry Mildmay, Bart. and Dame Jane his Wife, the FISHERY in the River called BURNHAM RIVER, otherwise WALL FLEET, extending from the West End of a certain Place there called CLAY-CLODS, to a Place called RAY SAND HEAD, and on the RAY-SAND, in the Main Sea, that an UNLAWFUL COMBINATION has been entered into by several Oyster Dredgers in and near Brightlingsea, for the Purpose of coming into the said Fishery, in a large Body, and by Force, dredging for Oysters therein, and carrying away the same, the Property of the said Hawkins and Co.

Notice is hereby given,

That the said Fishery is the undoubted Private Property of the said Sir H. Mildmay, and Dame Jane his Wife; and that the same hath been enjoyed by them and their Ancestors, without Interruption, from the Time of King Edward the First, by whom it was granted; and that all Persons who shall come into the said Fishery, and, by Force, dredge therein for Oysters, will be guilty of a MISDEMEANOUR, and will be punishable by Law accordingly. And if any Person or Persons, in a Body, or individually, shall, without Authority, attempt to dredge in the said Fishery for Oysters, he or they will be prosecuted for the same with the utmost Rigour of the Law.

Dated 16*th June,* 1806.

MEGGY, CHALK, AND CO. CHELMSFORD.

A warning against illegal oyster dredging in the approaches to the River Crouch, posted in 1806.

The Burnham men were, however, by now prepared, and 'provided with proper implements, cut away the dredges as fast as they were thrown overboard'. Seven men were committed to Chelmsford Goal. The naval brig *Turbulent* also appeared on the scene and as the smacks 'endeavoured to sail away, they were overhauled and several proper men were taken out for His Majesty's Service'.[6]

The chronicle of the oyster wars ends on an almost farcical note.

The lowest reach of the Blackwater estuary remained common ground, even after the formation of the Tollesbury and Mersea Oyster Co.; 'furriners' dredging brood here may not have been welcomed, but their rights were respected. But in the latter half of the ninteenth century Burnham boats made a practice of dredging up culch, and this was quite another matter, the equivalent of despoiling the seed corn, or more accurately the soil on which the seed corn had to grow. There was, however, no legal way to prevent it, so one day in 1894 the Tollesbury men took the law into their own hands.

Four Burnham boats were at work, all employed by James Wiseman of Paglesham, *Emmeline, Alma* (which had been chased away the previous week), *Wonder* and *Rose,* when three Tollesbury smacks, including *Express* and *Village Maid,* each carrying twenty or thirty men, confronted them. The master of the *Rose* produced a gun, which, though it was unloaded, enabled him to escape, but the other three were boarded and their culch thrown back on to the Bench Head. The *Emmeline* had 260 tubs, or over 700 bushels. Picturesque details include demands for tobacco and cocoa by the Tollesbury men and the playing of a tin whistle by one of the Burnham men.

As a result five Tollesbury men were charged that they 'did piratically and feloniously assault' the master of the *Emmeline,* and did 'piratically, feloniously and violently seize goods' from her. The case attracted 200 to Witham Court, where it was explained that the culch was to be taken into Burnham for sale after bleaching ashore. There was a little spat on it, which would of course have perished, and the Tollesbury men's lawyer showed his ignorance by explaining that they would 'make no complaint about taking culch, only brood', whereas the facts were the exact opposite. The Bench sent the first case for trial at the Assize, and the second was withdrawn, after the Burnham advocate had observed that he would withdraw both if the defendants would plead guilty, which they were in no mood to do.

Thanks to the extravagant wording of the charge, the affair gained great notoriety as The Piracy Case, the last of its kind, according to some, in English legal history. When it came to the Assize it attracted a distinctly Dickensian judge (Mr. Justice Day), who, arriving from Norfolk, got out of the train at Marks Tey in order to enter the county town riding horseback. He then proceeded to review his calendar, observing that 'the suggested charge of piracy on the high seas was a most trumpery one', which he proposed to treat with the contempt it deserved. When it came up for hearing on the second day, having already closed the jury's minds against the possibility of a real trial, he was as good as his word, with derisory references to 'scultch or whatever it is called', and the conclusion, based on the playing of the tin whistle, that all the parties 'parted the best of friends'. Declaring that he knew no precedent for 'such a scandalous abuse of the criminal law' he found all the prisoners not guilty and allowed them costs.[7]

Thus neither legal incompetence nor judicial pomposity contributed anything to the solution of a problem of vital importance to the oyster trade. Direct campaigning was, however, more effective. Public meetings were held in all the Colneside and Blackwater villages, and even in the Whitstable Oyster Company's Large Hall. Backed by this weight of opinion, representations to the Board of Trade (which at first resorted to the discredited and irrelevant notion of prohibiting all dredging of oysters and of culch from May to September) ultimately resulted in the Shell Fish Regulations Act, giving the Kent and Essex Sea Fisheries Committee powers to regulate and control the taking of culch from any grounds.

The Colne Fishery companies

The first Colne Fishery Co. came into existence in 1807, an association of the licensed dredgermen, not formally incorporated by statute or charter, but appointing two foremen, a treasurer and a clerk chosen by a jury at an Admiralty Court. It was a success, for by 1825 the fishery was in a more flourishing state than ever before.[1]

The Company's code of rules was recognised by Colchester Corporation in 1827, including powers to borrow up to £5,000 for purchase of brood and culch. By 1848 it was paying £600 a year rent to the Corporation, and valued its stock at £20,000, with annual sales from £1,000 to £5,000, while by 1861 the rent had increased by £150 a year, and the Company comprised 360 dredgermen, paying £2. 2s. each for licences for four dredges, based on ten shillings per dredge, with a sixpenny fee for the Town Clerk.

This progress seems to have continued smoothly till about 1865, when the Corporation decided to increase the licence fees, which had stood for 160 years. The dredgermen refused to pay and brought a test case.[2]

The Court of Common Pleas, in 1867, ruled that the Corporation had the right to grant, refuse or vary the terms of a licence, but urged 'the expediency of conciliating the inhabitants of the river banks' and suggested a solution by Act of Parliament. An appeal the following year again supported the Corporation.

The Act of Parliament which resulted, the Colne Fishery Act 1870, was thus born by compromise out of acrimony, an unhappy parentage for a misbegotten offspring. After dissolving the old company, and annulling the rules of 1827, it set up a new Colne Fishery Co., to consist of all those granted licences in 1867 and 1868, together thereafter with such others, residing in the eight Colneside parishes already mentioned, as should have served a seven-year apprenticeship and reached the age of twenty-one. To this Company the Corporation granted a ninety-nine-year lease in return for an annual rent of £500, a quarter of the profits of the oyster fishery, after allowing for an annual contribution of £1,500 to expenses, and half the profits from 'floating fish'.

But instead of being left to the Company, the management of the whole enterprise was entrusted to a Fishery Board, consisting of six members of the Company and six from the Corporation, with its own clerk, two treasurers and two auditors, one representing, in each case, the Company and the other the Corporation. This two-headed monster continued to preside over the affairs of the fishery, with the two interests in almost perpetual disagreement, throughout the entire ninety-three years of its existence.

The problems of the fishery's first forty years were set out by its chairman, Dr. Henry Laver, in an angry little pamphlet which he produced in 1914, attacking those who still wanted to revert to the pre-1870 system.[3] The views are coloured by the writer's frustration, but tell more about the fishery than the bland little official history he published two years later.[4] Amplifying 'a few remarks' he made, or attempted to make, at the close of the annual meeting, Laver writes:

'I took first the years from 1870, when the lease began, to 1888, and showed that the Corporation during this period entirely neglected

General map of the River Colne entrance and the adjoining creeks.

Rowhedge, Fingringhoe

Wivenhoe

Alresford Creek

North Geedon Creek

Rat Island

South Geedon Creek

Pyefleet Creek

Peewit Island

The Bracefleet

Modern Oysterage

Pyefleet Creek

The Strood

EAST MERSEA

West Marsh Point

BRIGHTLINGSEA

Cindery Islands

COLNE ESTUARY

Line of buoys marking fishery western limit

The Gazelett

Bench Head Shoal

Fishery Buoy

Colne Point

Nass Beacon

their duty and handed over the entire management to the company members of the Board, who kept the accounts, bought and sold as they pleased, and managed the fishery without even consulting the Corporation members, who acquiesced in this grave irregularity. I then called their attention to the results that showed that the income from sales was very small, not a tithe of what it might have been, and that it dwindled till in 1882 the whole sales from this fine fishery amounted to only £19 16s., and that the two years following, namely 1883 and 1884, were little better.' [They were in fact £318 and £975.]

'I then contrasted the amount paid for work in the fishery during the first nineteen years of the lease for catching in the river for Pyefleet, known generally as brooding, and also for preparing for market those taken for Pyefleet. Under the first heading . . . there was paid during the nineteen years £5,627. Catching and preparing for market for the same nineteen years amounted to £11,340. For the remaining years of the lease, from 1889 to 1913, during which time the Corporation has taken some share in the management, the amount paid under the same headings are for brooding £35,662, and catching and preparing for market £30,899, a total of £66,521 for the last twenty-five years as against only £16,968 for the first nineteen years.

'From 1870 to 1889 there were only about six years when a dividend was paid, the total being £5,551. The next twenty-five years the gross amount of dividend was £73,113'.

The dredgermen's opposition was based on their resentment at seeing 'their' fishery subsidise the ratepayers of Colchester, who in addition to rent were usually entitled to between £1,000 and £3,000 a year, the highest total, £5,891, being in 1895. But it is not easy to see what the final nett return amounted to, for, in Laver's words, 'members forget that the Corporation give considerable assistance by paying a portion of the expenses, for instance, a quarter of the expenses of culch, the expenses of the steam boats, part of the salaries of clerks and others, altogether amounting to a considerable sum yearly'.

Around 1880 regular monthly Board meetings began, but in addition the Company still held its own meetings, taking decisions and issuing cheques which it refused to divulge, and the Corporation also met separately. No conventional trading accounts were prepared, showing items such as depreciation of the value of stock. Instead the profits were distributed annually, with the result that purchases and even working expenses had to be financed by repeated borrowings, since the Act made no provision for working capital.

The dividends were, as Laver stated, negligible till 1889 but thereafter were substantial till 1903, often exceeding £5,000 and reaching £10,111 after the record profit of 1895, with widows entitled to participate. Nevertheless the Company members repeatedly clamoured for a bonus of £1 a head – a demand rejected as inadmissible under the Act, till in 1891 it was finally paid, but 'not as a precedent'. Applications for membership occupied much time at Board meetings, with nearly as many apprentices refused as were accepted in the early years. One applicant, J. H. Ham, threatened legal proceedings if he was rejected and in fact successfully appealed in 1899, leaving the Board with no alternative but to accept a member they thought 'quite unsuitable'.

Thanks to their long-standing resentment at the Corporation's intrusion into their affairs, the Company members showed little loyalty to the fishery. The 'flat grounds', as the Bench Head, off East Mersea, was called, were protected by a string of grapnels, extending to the Fishery Buoy opposite Colne Point; when these were lifted in 1889 they had caught many dredges identified as belonging to Company men, who were merely fined a day's pay. The watchmen, whom the Board insisted on appointing despite the claim of the Company to pick their pals, were clearly ineffective, till in 1891 they were first supplemented and then replaced by a river police force, described at the end of this chapter.

The Company men were also the Board's suppliers and competitors as well as its employees. They claimed preference when it came to buying brood, sometimes (according to Laver) cheating with stones and limpets at the bottom of the measure, and up to 1899 demanding the right to cull out oysters and charge for these separately at prices above the market rate. This was another bone of contention, for Laver noted in his pamphlet:

'There is no form of adding to the stock which has paid so well as buying large oysters to put at once into Pyefleet. It pays much better than the purchase of brood, as the death rate of this is so enormous, much exceeding fifty per cent. The purchase of ware arouses great opposition, but there was none shown when those bringing in broods were allowed to take the large oysters out, and were paid for these 8s. 4d. a hundred, when numbers were being sold from Pyefleet for seven shillings per hundred. This was the rule in 1890 and 1891. It would pay much better to give up the purchase of brood altogether and expend the money on the purchase of ware.'

In his journal Laver noted, 'the Company members have their own grounds, and take care that the Company and Corporation business shall not by its prosperity injure their own private business.' Yet when the Corporation members proposed to raise the selling price, the Company members usually refused, or proposed a reduction.

They also resisted the purchase of sufficient brood to enable the Company to fulfil its orders. As a result it was often sold out soon after Christmas, resulting not only in lost revenue, but more important in the loss of goodwill from customers who transferred their trade elsewhere. Nor would they agree to spend on advertising, with the result that 'Colchester never sells a single oyster in the large towns of the North and the Midlands'. For all these reasons Laver despaired of seeing Colchester ever rival Whitstable in prosperity. In some years, he observed, the Whitstable Company paid out more in dividend and loan reductions than Colchester's gross sales. Another factor (which interested him less) may have been that Whitstable also re-laid foreign oysters, which Colchester never did.

The antagonism between Corporation and Company members was becoming less marked by the time of Laver's death in 1917, but was at its height in 1891 when the Board had before it two proposals – to appoint a manager and to build a steam paddle dredger. The Corporation members favoured both; the Company members opposed them. As there was no provision for a casting vote the Board referred the decision to an arbitrator who decided in each case in favour, without giving reasons but with a bill for £116 for his time and trouble. (History nearly repeated itself with the decision to build the steam launch *Edward VII* in 1901. An identical dead-lock led to the Corporation members giving notice of arbitration, but this time the Company members withdrew their opposition.)

The manager chosen was Edgar Newman, who had been for sixteen years secretary of the Roach River Co., and who three years previously had made an interesting report on the Colne. He found the grounds free of pests, but with much of the culch covered with mud through lack of cultivation. He criticised the custom of taking so much brood into Pyefleet, pointing out that young stock should be left about the grounds to spat. He also disapproved of wire riggings on dredges used on breeding grounds, and found fault with the clumsy dredge warps used, which were cast-offs from the deep-sea smacks, 'serviceable in the North Sea but quite unsuited to the river'.

As a result of this inspection Newman must have been known to most of the dredgermen, yet when he attended his first meeting in 1892 the Company men protested that a stranger was present. When he was introduced as their manager they declared he certainly was not, and walked out. This attitude was not confined to the privacy of the monthly meetings. The annual meetings, held in Colchester Town Hall, were fully reported in the local press. In 1907 after a favourable report on progress and prospects, a Company member, Charles Brasted, observed, 'If they put the manager into the foreman's place for a month he would be dead. The manager came down like a toff and there was a nice steamboat waiting for him. He had a gentleman's life.' The chairman then proceeded to the election of twelve members, of whom six were to be accepted for the Board, prefacing this with the formal inquiry whether any non-members were present. To which Brasted gracefully responded, 'Hop it, Newman. Out you go!'[5]

Despite these rebuffs, Newman guided the fishery through its most prosperous years till 1905, when he was succeeded by G.L. Trussell, who had also been secretary of the Roach River Co.

With demand exceeding supply every season, foreign orders were usually rejected. On several occasions it was decided that inquiries from Ostend and Yserke, in Holland, should 'lie on the table'. In 1894, however, some oysters were returned from Ostend as unsatisfactory. It was pointed out that as they were green they could not have come from Colchester, but instead of leaving it at that Newman offered to lay them in the Colne and replace them the following year. He then made a visit to Ostend, accompanied by a Corporation member of the Board, who reported on the good impression created and the interest of merchants who hitherto had hardly heard of the Colchester fishery and believed it to be a new enterprise. As a result a big European trade developed, extending to Russia, and in 1898, when the stock in the river was estimated at nine million, Newman was able to recommend buying as much brood as could be found to meet the English and foreign markets. No doubt the Company members disagreed, for in 1894, when he had asked for £10,000 for this purpose the Corporation members had suggested £5,000 and the Company members rejected any expenditure at all – a typical example of what the poor man had to put up with.

He was again championing expansion in 1901 with an imaginative project which never came to fruition. Observing that the fishery only had sufficient pits on Peewit Island for the winter storage of one-third of its three million stock, with no room to dig more, he proposed to hire the Langenhoe marshes between Pyefleet and the Geedons Creeks (now known as Rat Island) to dig pits there for another million. But he went

Culling oysters for market, Colne Oyster Fishery, c.1900.

further with a plan to double the capacity of Pyefleet by hiring the Corporation's steam bucket dredger to clear away the mud from the upper end, a task too much for the paddle dredger *Pyefleet*. To handle the projected stock of six million oysters he proposed a new double packing house on Rat Island, with new hards giving access to both Pyefleet and the river. The Company members put the boot in, opposing every aspect of the scheme. Oysters laid so far up the creek would 'green' they declared – something the manager admitted had been noticed in the past.

Five years after the arbitrator had approved the idea of a steam dredger, the *Pyefleet* was commissioned at a cost of £471, two-thirds contributed by the Company and one-third by the Corporation. The Company members celebrated the occasion by finding fault with her, maintaining that she would not steam slowly enough for dredging. The whole Board went afloat for a test, when it was found that she could steam with her paddles turning as slowly as twelve revolutions per minute. At 14 r.p.m. she towed eight dredges on the tide, and all came up half full except one which was on its back. Despite this, when the *Pyefleet* went to Aldous's yard for a refit the following year, a yacht was promptly put behind her so she was beneaped and could not be re-launched for a fortnight, to the open delight of the Company members.

These ructions occurred at the height of the new Company's prosperity. Following the great spatfall of 1858, sales had reached £18,000, with £17,000 and £16,000 in the two following years, but ten years later the boom had passed.[6] John Smith of Burnham told the 1883 Blackwater inquiry it was in decline through bad management, and that he had offered £700 a year to hire it. It was, however, put back on its feet by another big spatfall in 1881 and then enjoyed nearly half a century of success. The most profitable year in its history was 1895, when it sold 2,733,115 oysters at the high

The steam paddle dredger Pyefleet, built by Forrest and Co. of Wivenhoe for the Colchester Oyster Fishery Co.

The ceremonial hauling of the first dredge of a new oyster season, Colchester Oyster Fishery, early 20th century.

price of 19 shillings per hundred, giving gross sales of £26,061, and a profit to the Fishery Company of £13,767 of which £5,891 accrued to Colchester Corporation.[7]

Sales exceeded three million from 1898 to 1901 inclusive, again in 1913, and from 1924 to 1928 inclusive, but at lower prices. Up to 1928, with the exception of three major slumps, sales fluctuated between one and three million, the profit to the Company ranging from £1,000 to £9,000, and the selling price from eight to 18 shillings a hundred, till it exceeded £1 a hundred in 1923 and thereafter soared in a vain effort to make the best of dwindling yields.

The first slump came in 1892 when sales fell from 1,150,550 in the previous year to a mere 322,012, with a further decline to 105,950 in 1893 and a recovery to 675,040 in 1894. In the two latter years the price rose to 23 shillings a hundred, but even so in 1893 the Company lost £2,563 and the Corporation for the first time received no share of profit. This setback was presumably connected with the cholera outbreak of 1893 and the 'oyster scare' associated with Dr. Bulstrode's report in 1896, but it would seem that the public had already been frightened off oysters, and it is surprising that sales recovered to over 2,700,000 in 1895 (the year of record profits) and again in 1896, with no apparent reaction to the report in the following years.

The second slump was in 1903, when sales plunged from 2,218,874 to 282,662, clearly as the result of the Emsworth poisoning disaster. They recovered to over one-and-three-quarter million in 1904 and 1905, but prices were now lower (11s. 8d. down to 7s. 8d.) and the Company again lost money, though Colchester Corporation received £1,256 in 1904 and £498 in 1905.

The third slump reduced sales from over two-and-a-half million in 1914 to 771,117 in 1915, presumably the effect of the war on exports, though turnover then returned to normal for the remaining war years and the fishery later received £3,000 compensation from the Admiralty for war-time damage. Colchester Corporation helped themselves to £1,000 of this.

The terminal decline set in in the 1920s when all the Essex and Kent fisheries were affected by troubles – perhaps virus diseases introduced by increased shipping movements from foreign waters, perhaps industrial pollution – which have never been fully explained or understood, and from which they were never to recover.

Sales fell below half a million in 1930 and below a quarter million in 1933, continuing a steady downward trend with only a slight recovery in 1947 (253,830) and from 1954 to 1956 (upwards of a quarter million annually). Prices were raised to unheard-of levels, exceeding 30 shillings a hundred in 1927, £3 in 1936 and £5 in 1948, when the fishery received its Admiralty compensation for World War II damage of £2,000, of which Colchester Corporation grabbed £1,507.

The affairs of the fishery reflect these trends. Optimism was high enough in 1901 for a second steam dredger to be proposed, and in 1906 the packing sheds on Peewit Island were extended. This positive, progressive outlook lasted till the First World War, but after it the picture changed sharply.

Slipper limpets had made their appearance in 1912 and now became a major problem. In the twelve years to 1924 three thousand tons were cleared off the fishery, and in the five years to 1930 no fewer than 3,564 tons. They had to be laid ashore and their bleached shells then served for culch, but by the end of the war the Mersea Shell Crushing Co. provided a modest revenue. Limpets were an enemy which ingenuity and hard work could fight, but the mysterious mortality which struck in 1920 and again in 1921 defied explanation or remedy, though for a while it was blamed on the dumping of war-time munitions at sea, perhaps in the hope of extracting compensation from the Government.

From this time onward, expansionist developments gave place to enforced economies. In 1923 it was agreed that the next two river police to retire should not be replaced and all-round wage cuts were proposed, though in the end only the dredgermen, who were paid £2 14s. a week, suffered a reduction to 9 shillings a day. (Pre-war they had earned 4s. 6d. a day.) Yet the Board still had the confidence to replace the *Pyefleet* in 1929. The thirty-three-year old paddler now required patches on her bottom to keep her afloat, and something more powerful than a smack was necessary to keep the grounds in order. An engine for the *Native* was suggested, but it was thought that at the age of twenty-five she was too old (though in fact she was fitted with a 28 h.p. paraffin motor in 1945), after which no-one could suggest any improvement on an exact replica of the old steamer, machinery and all.

The *Pyefleet II* was built at Rowhedge Ironworks, with machinery by Mumford's, for £3,050 – nearly seven times the cost of her predecessor. The project was not even controversial, beyond an amendment by the Brightlingsea-based Company members to accept Aldous's tender, which was £50 higher, and a protest at the use of a boiler from King's Lynn, though neither of the Colchester firms would quote for one. The *Pyefleet I* went to May and Butcher, the Heybridge breakers, for £42.

It was not a good investment, for the *Pyefleet II* was laid up in 1932, and though she was commissioned in 1934 for three weeks to work with a harrow on breaking up blubber, she was then put up for sale and knocked down to Joshua Francis, the Colchester barge-owner for £125. The Company members with long memories reminded the Board that they had never been in favour of her in the first place, and also took the opportunity to produce a petition by 124 members to get rid of the manager. The Corporation members resisted this but closed the office on North Hill, Colchester, moving both manager and office to a house in Brightlingsea, and sacking his clerk. They also offered an interest-free loan and a contribution of £50 as a quarter of the cost of catching limpets. In fact Mr. Trussell continued to manage to his death in 1933, completing twenty-eight years' service. He was never replaced, so that in all its ninety years the Company only had two managers.

After this little bit of bickering, however, the Corporation-Company antipathy was largely ended by the over-riding challenge of hard times. The Company members sought to extend the Corporation's grant for cleaning to cover catching, on the ground that any dredging included an element of cultivation, and this was accepted by the Corporation members, who would have rejected it out of hand half a century before. In 1935 the Company members actually carried a vote of thanks to the Corporation for its 'assistance over the last year or two', and in 1940 offered to forego the boat hire for the *Native* or the motor skiff now employed.

But troubles continued to multiply. The disastrous winter of 1939-40 left 1,500 oysters dead in the pits and destroyed 75 per cent of the marketable oysters throughout the fishery. A proposal in 1939 by the Chairman (Alderman, later Sir, Gurney Benham, my father, who I recall found this among the most bewildering of his public duties) to lay Brittany oysters, doubtless in imitation of the Tollesbury and Mersea Company's initiative, does not seem to have been adopted.

The fishery somehow surmounted the problems of the Second World War, when the possibility of having to employ unapprenticed labour was considered but apparently not adopted. It was, however, enfeebled with yet more problems to face.

In 1944 there was not enough work to go round, even for the reduced labour force, and it was agreed to employ the Company men by rotation, each working for one week, with a guaranteed payment for three days if weather made a full week's work impossible. The pre-war smack fleet was now a thing of the past, and the Admiralty's compensation money was spent partly on culch and partly on a new motor skiff. The boats hired in 1952 were thus the new skiff at £10 a week, the motorised *Native* and the skiff *Pyefleet* (still employed at West Mersea by Peter French) at eight guineas, and the old skiff *Economy* at £5.

The East Coast floods of 1953 inundated Peewit Island, damaging the packing sheds and washing away gear to the extent of £2,060, towards which the Lord Mayor's Relief Fund made a grant of £1,835. Two years later the repaired sheds were burned down – hopelessly under-insured, along with a lot of gear which was not insured at all – at a cost to the Board of over £1,000.

Shell disease was detected for the first time in 1952 and, though this remained a threat and cause of anxiety rather than a major problem, the mortality, which had been periodical, absent one winter and all too evident the next, was severe in 1956 and again in 1959, when it was aggravated by accumulations of mud, blamed on the increase in shipping using the river, though twenty years of inadequate cleaning must have had something to do with it.

In 1955 the Fishmongers Company condemned a sample of Colne oysters causing the immediate postponement of the official opening ceremony, due in a few days' time. Some years before this a case of typhoid in Colchester Isolation Hospital had been traced to Brightlingsea oysters, as a result of which the merchants there had installed a purifying tank, which in 1951, as the Brightlingsea and Tendring Shellfish Committee, they had offered to make available. Yet now, faced with a new deadly danger, the Board could propose nothing better than a storage tank 'above high water level', and as late as 1962, when the Burnham-on-Crouch Fishery Laboratory called their attention to the ultra-violet purification plant at Brightlingsea they resolved to 'consider other methods'.

By 1947 there were only four full-time workers eligible for holiday pay, and three casuals were laid off. The supply of No.1s was quite inadequate, and the fishery usually sold out by January or February and in 1958 by November. At the end of the 1954 selling season just 3,000 No.1s were left in Pyefleet, which it was proposed should be kept for stock, but they had to be sold. Baxter's, the London agents, needed 4,000 a day and could only be supplied with 2,000. Orders from Paris were turned down without even quoting. No.2s and No.3s were available, but of poor quality, with no demand for them. A good spatfall in 1959 raised some hope and justified the purchase of a thousand bushels of culch, probably the last laid. The *Native* was converted in 1956 for power dredging, using a 'diving dredge' developed at the Burnham Laboratory, which was found to increase catching by a quarter.

But there was little left to catch and little chance of the new spat reaching

COLNE FISHERY BOARD.

Notice is Hereby Given
THAT THE

SHIFTING OF THE STOCK

From the River to the Pyefleet fattening Ground, will commence on

MONDAY, the 9th MARCH, 1914,
WEATHER PERMITTING.

When Dredging is to commence and cease.

All boats are to be at the <u>appointed place</u> on the Fishery namely at the lower part of the River on the flood tide, and at the upper part on the ebb tide, <u>and ready to commence work at 7 o'clock a.m.</u> This rule must be strictly adhered to.

The Flag will be hoisted on board the Foreman's Smack for dredging to commence. The Flag will then be lowered, and at the proper time hoisted again for dredging to cease, when the boats will come and anchor near the flag boat, deliver their catch, and remain anchored until the flag is lowered, for the boats to leave the Fishery.

If any boats remain on the Fishery for the night, the crews must not leave the boats until the Flag is lowered, and such boats must not be anchored on any part of the East shore, where they are likely to ground at Low water.

Equipment of Boats.

All boats must be supplied with proper dredging gear, namely dredges of from seventeen to twenty pounds weight, warps not less than eighteen fathoms in length, and the rings on the wire rigging of the dredges to be two inches in diameter. Nets or baskets must be supplied to hold the catch. Bags will not be permitted. Small cull-knives must be supplied for culling the stuff.

Attention to Work.

Each Freeman is to keep constantly singling the Brood, whether there is a breeze or not, and in case of very little wind to row his smack so as to get sufficient for singling purposes. When clearing his deck of culch and stuff to be very careful not to deposit it on dirty ground or on the upper part of the shores. The boats must not work on the East shore during low water, and should any boat ground on the stuff through negligence the day's pay of the boat and men will be stopped.

Destruction of Vermin.

It is absolutely necessary to save out all limpets, fivefingers, tingles, mussels, and any rubbish injurious to the ground, and deposit same in the skiff which will be anchored in the River for that purpose.

Any dredgerman refusing to comply with this regulation will be reported to the Board for such negligence.

Crew for Steamdredger.

No boats will be allowed to work until the crew of the Steamdredger is complete.

BY ORDER,
GEORGE L. TRUSSELL, Manager.

WILES & SON, PRINTERS, COLCHESTER.

Notice of the shifting of stock by the Colne Oyster Fishery, 1914.

maturity. In 1952 the Company had urged the Corporation to increase its £1,500 allowance for cultivation; the Corporation members replied that they could not do this under the Fishery Act of 1870, but offered to forego their share of profit and to provide a £500 loan. By 1958 a deficit of £1,900 was forecast for the year to the following July, and the Corporation offered £1,500 if the Company would contribute £500.

Then came the death blow in the form of the terrible winter of 1962-3. When the ice cleared and the boats could get back on to the grounds, the mortality was at first put at seventy per cent, but soon it was recognised as a wipe-out, with only one per cent of the oysters surviving, many in a dying state. Four thousand survivors were gathered into Pyefleet, of which one thousand were reserved for the Colchester Oyster Feast. The Corporation members were asked for another loan to see the undertaking through to the end of its ninety-nine-year lease due to expire in 1969, but refused and proposed to surrender the lease. There was wistful talk of raising a £10,000 loan (but from whom, for the Company had few assets, no capital and no funds of any kind?) and employing three men with one boat in the hope of resuming limited trading in 1966, and full production in 1969, tiding over the intervening years by re-laying Portuguese oysters.

But the fishery was finished and the decision to close it was taken on 8 May 1963. Up to the very end the freemen of the river were presenting their sons for apprenticeship; only a few weeks before the final closure the indentures of John Death were approved, and an application to apprentice George Martin accepted – the last of a long line, and the end of a historic tradition. The Fishery Board held its last meeting in February 1964.

Before proceeding to consider the next chapter in the fishery's affairs, in private hands, some further aspects of the story remain to be described.

The Colne had its own customs and traditions. The Company only owned a couple of smacks, the *Native*, which was used as the foreman's flagship, to which catches were delivered, and which survived till the fishery closed, and the *Pyefleet*, which was condemned in 1917 to join the wrecks forming a breakwater on Peewit Island.[8] The Board hired these from the Company and all the other smacks from its members, originally at £1 a week, raised to £1 5s. in 1889. There were in that year forty-two such smacks, employing 118 men, operated in rotation, twelve at a time, working a six-hour day, with five hours on Friday. In 1892 the day was 7 a.m. to 3 p.m. or on one o'clock tides ceasing at high water. Work started and ended with the hoisting of a flag; if a smack was not ready when the flag went up she lost a day's work, and if she was seen idling before it was raised again, she was reported to the Board.

In later years more smacks were employed, for in 1912 'the whole fleet' of 40 smacks was put to work, along with the *Pyefleet*, clearing a ton of five-fingers off the Binnaker, and one of the periodical inspections by the Board in 1922 noted twenty-three smacks at work. By 1938, when the inspection noted only eleven smacks, the terms of employment included a payment of four shillings per 100 oysters, first and second size, with a condition that at least three wash of limpets be saved, for which an extra sixpence per man and boat was paid. For smacks with more than four hands there was an extra payment of a shilling a day, presumably an addition to the boat hire.

This system is more clearly shown by the notice posted before the shifting of stock started in May 1940, when the inspection noted only three boats at work. The boat hire then was six shillings a day for four-handed smacks, with one shilling extra for each dredge over four; five shillings for three-handed, and four shillings for two-handed boats, including fuel for motors. A wage of five shillings a day was paid, with the same payments for oysters caught and for the obligatory minimum three wash of limpets. The flag was hoisted at 8 a.m. and work ceased at 1.30. Smacks were required to anchor to deliver their catch and not to leave until cleared by police. They had to have dredges of eighteen to twenty pounds weight, with warps not less than eighteen fathoms long, and wire riggings at least two-inch gauge. Limpets had to be declared, not dumped, and all rubbish saved up and brought to the foreman. Brood had to be singled, and care taken that culch was not thrown overboard on the shores. The rules concluded: 'No single-handed smacks will be allowed to work'.

Apart from such glimpses as this, the actual earnings are difficult to follow, for the rates were constantly being changed, no doubt reflecting the right of the Company members to regulate their own affairs, unlike the employees of the more conventionally commercial companies, and because the different seasonal trades were treated and even costed separately, perhaps because cultivation attracted grants and loans from the Corporation as owners of the grounds being maintained and improved.

During the cleaning season the smacks were sometimes set to work using dredges with the bottom thong removed, so that the dredge caught nothing but raked and harrowed. They were then only allowed two-man crews. But smacks alone could not keep the extensive grounds clean, and it was for this that the *Pyefleet* was required and chiefly used, sometimes towing two harrows and two deep-sea dredges. In the spring the fleet spent a few weeks shifting stock from the river into Pyefleet for the summer fattening – an operation misleadingly called 'brooding'. After some more cleaning or a little final catching the boats were then dismissed for the summer. In the autumn came the catching, both in the river and in Pyefleet. This was often on a basis called 'stinting', with a daily or weekly 'stint' fixed by the Board. But as it was agreed in 1890 that men working on 'stint' should be paid £1 a week, this was not a piece-work payment, or a production bonus, but a minimum requirement to earn a wage. In 1890 the 'stint' was six wash one peck per week, and later the same year, when twenty boats were put to work on 'The Shelf', it was fixed at one peck per man per day. Between seasons the men were stood off, but they could still go to work on the common grounds, catching brood or dredging culch, to sell to the Company or elsewhere.

These earnings, while not lavish, were probably better than other companies paid and up to the end of the fishery efforts were made to keep
adding a few shillings a week. In 1943, when the foreman was earning
£3 7s. a week and the dredgermen 10 shillings a day, all were increased by
3 shillings a week, and by 1951 the dredging rate was 17 shillings a day,
with a bonus of 2 shillings per hundred oysters in the catching season, later
changed to 5 shillings for every fifty No. 1s in excess of the first fifty, the
bonus to be shared equally between all crews, 'including engineers'. At the
last increase in 1962 the dredgermen were raised from £8 15s. to £9 10s. a
week, the foreman from £10 3s. 6d. to £11, and the 'engineers' from £8 19s.
to £9 14s.

The Colne River Police, started in 1891 as a result of the watchmen's in-
ability to control poaching (often by Company members) or even to keep
awake during the night, were a feature of the fishery for half a century, patrolling day and night and attending to oversee the delivery of smacks'
'stints' at the end of each day's work. Their first H.Q. was the hospital ship
which lay in the Colne for quarantine purposes up to the start of the First
World War, but later they were based in Brightlingsea. They were part of
the Colchester Borough police force but three-quarters of the cost was paid
by the Fishery. A member of the County Police, Thomas Poole, was
appointed to take charge with the rank of sergeant. Under him were three
constables, with a steam launch, *Viking*, and two sailing boats specially
built at Rowhedge, *Alert* and *Brisk*. *Viking* was replaced in 1902 by a much
grander steam launch, *Edward VII*, which was converted to motor power
with a 50h.p. Britannia engine in 1913[9]. After various breakages and break-
downs this was declared beyond repair within a few years, leaving the
police to depend on their sailing fleet, which was the admiration of
yachtsmen, as well as the pride of the police, for half a century. The boats,
all centre-board, half-decked sloops, with big loose-footed gaff mainsails
and jibs set flying on short bowsprits, included *Raven, Colne, Victoria,
Alexandra* and *Prince of Wales*. The later craft were mostly built by Aldous at
Brightlingsea, and their quality may have owed something to Tom Poole's
eye for a boat. Within living memory all had small cabins, just big enough
to contain bogy stoves, for which 'Smithy coal' was stored in a shed on
Peewit Island, close to the headquarters of the oyster fishery. They were
painted grey, including the decks, with teak brown coamings and cabin-
sides.[10]

Sailed single-handed, they were immacuately kept and smartly handled, with their crews maintaining a discipline which would not have dis-
graced the Brigade of Guards. There was always one boat (and in earlier
years sometimes two) patrolling the estuary, day and night, making a
'point' with the sergeant every two hours, usually at Bateman's Tower on
the end of the Promenade. The duty changes were timed to a minute. In
strong winds the boat would sail into Brightlingsea Creek, where the
relieving officer rowed off to her, jumping aboard as the other policeman
stepped into his boat to come ashore. In calms, when there was not enough

Mersea and Maldon smacks racing. Fishing under sail and in particular the close manoeuvre during much oyster dredging developed ability and aptitude for yacht racing. Many racing captains and crews came from the fishing communities of the Colne and Blackwater.

wind to sail, the duty boat lay at anchor off East Mersea, her mainsail tack traced up the mast, her gaff rucked down, with the halyard frapped round the sail.

A police regatta was an annual event in the early years, with Town Councillors and Fishery Board members present in force aboard the fishery's steam paddle dredger, *Pyefleet*. The event in August 1896 included rowing and sculling races, with men from the town police force unsuccessfully challenging their maritime colleagues, and water frolics including a Water Derby, in which the policemen mounted barrels fitted with horses' heads and tails and paddled to a prize or a ducking. In the police boats' race, the course was twice round Rat Island, and the winner was the scratch boat *Colne*, with *Alert* and *Raven* second and third.

Tom Poole was himself a keen yachtsman. He bought *Victoria* for his own use, but was best known at Brightlingsea with his *Valiant*, which he sailed in local races for thirty-three years, wearing a stiff winged collar afloat just as he did ashore. He was promoted Inspector in 1898, but in retirement always referred to himself as 'the former Superintendent of the River Police'. He also succeeded to the title of Water Bailiff.

By 1919 the Force comprised one Superintendent, three Sergeants and ten Constables, of whom the Superintendent, one Sergeant and three Constables were full members of the Borough Police, with the remainder retained by the Fishery. Pay increases in that year led to a reduction, with the Superintendent and two Constables on the Borough strength and two Sergeants and four Constables retained by the Fishery.

The River Police were suspended in 1942, a war-time measure which became permanent, though several of the old fleet, including *Colne* and *Prince of Wales,* survived as yachts. Some of the men came ashore and took on more mundane duties in Colchester. I recall one of them on point duty at Headgate in the days before traffic lights. Bicycling to my office I could be sure of a cheery sailorman's greeting as he waved me round the corner – 'Hard a-port!', 'Bear away there!', or usually 'Keep her full, boy!'.

CHAPTER FIFTEEN

Enclosing the Blackwater

The enclosure of most of the common land in England went on over six centuries, reaching its climax in the eighteenth century, when between 1760 and 1797 some 1,500 private Enclosure Acts passed through Parliament, some to serve the greed of rapacious landowners, others in the interests of improved agriculture and job prospects.

Oystermen faced a comparable change in their way of life a century later, with a great spawning of companies in the mid-nineteenth century. Up to the passing of the Sea Fisheries Act of 1866 an Act of Parliament was required, but thereafter the process was simplified and encouraged, for the Board of Trade would grant a 'Several Order' to enclose grounds and to confer powers to regulate them. It was the age when 'capital' was accepted as the panacea for all evils and the source of all progress, much as nationalisation and then privatisation have been embraced in our times. Capital would provide resources, produce development, increase employment, permit organisation – all conspicuous by their absence in the happy-go-lucky hunting grounds of the free fisheries, where hundreds of dredger-men picked up such living as they could from whatever nature provided, putting back nothing in return beyond the actual working of their dredges, the importance of which was often overlooked, for in the long term under-fishing could be as damaging as over-fishing on fertile grounds.

The Blackwater estuary was a tempting prize – the finest oyster nursery in the country and 'definitely superior to the Colne', according to Edward Stammers of Brightlingsea. Moreover, the estuary had seen a huge spatfall in 1858 which was worked out by the early 1860s, so it then presented a copybook example of decay and decline due to unregulated over-fishing, comparing unfavourably with the company-controlled Colne and Crouch.

The issue came to a head with an application in 1867 for enclosures by three companies – the Fish and Oyster Breeding Co., whose story has been told in an earlier chapter, the Blackwater Oyster Fishing Co., formed by R. Page of Bradwell with his brother as partner, and the Maldon Native Oyster Fishery Ltd., established in 1862, which asked for a mile of ground between Mill Point and Shingle Head. These two companies claimed a capital of £25,000 and £20,000 respectively (the sort of notional figure which seems to have been usual to obtain credibility), but in the case of the Maldon Native Co. it was 'not at present subscribed', and in the case of the Blackwater Fishing Co., 'some £5 shares had been allotted on five shilling deposits'. The three applicants regarded themselves as complementary rather than competitive, issuing a joint circular, since each wanted a different area, the exact extent of which is not clear since the all-important map does not survive.

The applications were heard at a great Board of Trade public inquiry at Maldon, which had to transfer to the Public Hall because of an attendance of 500 dredgermen. It continued for three days, was adjourned for a month and then resumed for several more days, with the same full house for every sitting.

All the applications were based on the assumption that company control was the natural order of progress. 'The parallel is between hand loom weaving and machinery, or stage coaches and railways', it was claimed. But not all the witnesses were so sanguine. Edward Stammers pointed to companies at Faversham, Rochester, Milton and Queenborough – all gone. 'I knew two at Orford, both gone', he added. John Solly made it clear that after his experience with the Tollesbury Oyster Co., he had had enough of companies. Most of the dredgermen's objections were less articulate expressions of fear and dislike at the prospect of losing their rights. One man observed, 'I don't know the Colne would be in any worse state without the company'[1].

Estimates of possible future employment were blindly optimistic. Francis Francis, a former manager of the Jersey Fisheries, said the river could employ 1,200 men at 18 shillings a week, and other advocates claimed wages would rise to £1 a week with a thousand men employed all the year round.

I have not traced the report of the inspector's findings, but it seems clear that only the Fish and Breeding Co. was approved, perhaps because part of its ground had been previously leased by Maldon Corporation. Its fishery was in fact 'the first established under the new system' (that is, 'the several orders' already mentioned).

Not content with this success, the Company applied in 1875 to extend 'the finest layings in the kingdom' down river to take in part of the common ground. This resulted in a stormy meeting of 200 dredgermen, presided over by Dr. J. H. Salter of Tolleshunt D'Arcy, at which it was again argued that the unprotected Blackwater was badly fished out and that only a company could re-stock it with brood and control its use. A shareholding system was proposed, based on that of the Emsworth company, which would give half the control to the dredgermen owning £5 'A' shares, for which they need only subscribe a shilling deposit, paying off the rest from profits, while 5,000 'B' shares, fully paid up, would provide £25,000 of much needed working capital.[1]

But was that worth the sacrifice of 'inalienable rights'? It was perceptively observed that there was nothing in the 'A' shareholding system to prevent ownership falling into one or two hands, and that 'if local men could keep our brood and spat it would conserve our river'. In due course these misgivings were to prove correct, as both control and spat passed to Kentish interests. Sometimes there were 300 sail in the river; could the Company pay wages for so many? Wivenhoe, Brightlingsea and Rowhedge would be shut out.

The Mersea men had already met and agreed to join with Brightlingsea in opposition, 'as they did in 1863' (so evidently the 1867 applications had cast a long shadow before them). Mr. Solly of the Tollesbury Oyster Co. moved rejection, and at the end of an incoherent meeting this was carried with only one dissentient. The Tollesbury men, however, did not vote. Instead they returned home, held another meeting at which they decided that the Mersea men were 'snakes in the grass', with plans for an application of their own, and voted to approve the Maldon offer![2]

At the end of the mass meeting, Dr. Salter, who was probably quite accustomed to this sort of performance, observed that it had cleared the air, which may indeed have been the case, for within a year local antipathies had been overcome – by whose initiative or diplomacy it would be interesting to know – and the Tollesbury and Mersea (Blackwater) Oyster Co. Ltd. had been formed.[3] This made application for a 'Several Order' in 1877. The Board of Trade inquiry was less colourful than the earlier meeting, but more constructive.[4]

John Smith's Maldon Fish and Breeding Co. did not renew its application, perhaps because he already had plans to establish himself as the controlling shareholder of the Tollesbury and Mersea venture. Three other companies, however, put forward proposals, and a Brightlingsea non-conformist minister, Rev. J. Deans, was given permission to represent a Brightlingsea and Wivenhoe Dredgermen's Defence Committee, of which he was secretary, though he does not seem to have summoned up the courage to say anything.

The exact nature of the three companies and the extent of the grounds they sought are once again not entirely clear. The Bradwell Oyster Fishery Co. Ltd. was apparently a consortium of local landowners, who claimed manorial rights over the river opposite Peewit Island, but refused to reveal details of them because they were contested by Maldon Corporation. The Blackwater River Oyster Fishery Co. Ltd. applied for a small area of 100 acres, proposing to spend £10,000, 'which must benefit the remaining 10,000 acres of public ground', while the St. Peter's (Blackwater) Oyster Co. Ltd. proposed to spend the same amount, presumably on another patch. Both these companies claimed the support of Mr. James Wiseman, who was chairman and manager of the Blackwater Co., though his connection with the St. Peter's Company is not clear. It was stated that he and his colleagues had invested £25,000 in the Roach, without return, for four or five years, but that this had since become profitable and that Wiseman also owned beds in the Crouch, 'Mersea Creek' and the Blackwater. The Tollesbury and Mersea Company's claim was for 2,678 acres, including all the grounds sought by their competitors, who poured scorn on the idea of a co-operative organisation finding the capital for so large a project. But the T. & M. had strong backing. Tollesbury, with a population of 1,500, had 300 dredgermen, owning 70 smacks; East and West Mersea, with a similar population, had 120 dredgermen with 47 smacks (of which one was based at East Mersea) and all these, without a single dissentient, had agreed to become 'A' shareholders, offering a prospect of £30,000 capital in 3,000 each of 'A' and 'B' shares.

There was no disagreement as to the need for some control. A great spat-fall in 1858 had attracted boats from all round the country. The Bradwell coastguard remembered 400 working the river in that year, but for the past few years had only seen forty or fifty. Even the Brightlingsea and Wivenhoe men had now deserted it. (Forty smacks under sail, regarded as derisory, must have been a brave sight; the thought of 400 beggars imagination.) The choice lay between the experienced professionals from Paglesham, who could offer a proven record of success, and the idealistic aim of producing co-operation among the 400 dredgermen of Tollesbury and Mersea, who had the prior claim by right. The Board of Trade were prepared to take the long view, and the T. & M. started operations two years later, with what results we shall see in the next chapter.

First, however, before leaving the story of the long arguments over the enclosure of the Blackwater, we may conveniently consider its final chapter.

The Tollesbury and Mersea Company's grant left only the lowest reach of the river, off Mersea Island, as common ground. This was soon being sought after by the acquisitive John Smith of Burnham and by the Colneside oyster villages which continued to feel that they had been shut out of the great Blackwater nursery.

The two claims were heard before a Board of Trade inquiry in 1883, with the T. & M. itself remaining neutral.[5] Smith, already a major shareholder in the T. & M., explained that he did not want to work the lower Blackwater himself, but if he won the concession he would add it to the T. & M. grounds, in return for which he expected 1500 £5 'A' shares and 1500 'B' shares. This bare-faced scheme had not even been agreed by the T. & M. and the Inspector had no hesitation in throwing it out.

The Colneside application was from the Brightlingsea, Wivenhoe, and East Donyland Co-operative Oyster Fishery, a concern dreamed up in 1882 by the Rev. J. Deans, apparently replacing an earlier Defence Committee. An enthusiastic amateur expert, he appeared in person and got his leg pulled for his pains. His company, modelled on the T. & M., had 'A' and 'B' shares, for which in the first month £5,375 and £13,025 respectively were subscribed. By the time of the inquiry the capital was £40,000.[6]

The report of the hearing provides a delightful picture of the bucolic life of the flatsmen. One counsel appeared to represent 538 poor but honest dredgers of Mersea and Tollesbury, owning 103 smacks who in the past twelve months had gathered eight and a half million spat worth, at three shillings a hundred, £12,750. These men owned small smacks which could not voyage far afield, unlike the Colne boats. Tollesbury had by this time ninety-two small (Class 2) smacks and four Class 1; Mersea thirty-nine and only one big vessel. Samuel Musset had two smacks, one of six tons and one of nine; his family owned eight, all built for the river. Willoughby John Bean, manager to Henry May, one of the biggest Mersea laying-owners, said he relied on the flatsmen, particularly since the T. & M. had refused to honour an undertaking to sell him brood.

Most of the men, including some who owned smacks, relied on picking up spat and brood by hand. Abraham Green of West Mersea said he picked up winkles, oysters, lobsters, eels and whelks. With his three teenage sons he could earn £2 a week. He had five other children and they, their mother and her sisters all went on the mud. He knew because he had to fit them out with splashers. His only boat was a punt, and his stock-in-trade was an eel spear, a pair of splashers and a basket. Plus, he added, a second basket for winkles. It is difficult to picture a greater contrast to the swashbuckling way of life of the Swin rangers and Channel-bashers.

The Co-operative Oyster Fishery's application was refused and the Company was at once wound up. It would seem that in the Blackwater officialdom got the balance about right between controlled cultivation and free exploitation, but the Vicar of Brightlingsea was still fulminating ten years later, recalling that his flock 'should be allowed some of the pickings that have fallen so abundantly to West Mersea and Tollesbury'.

'The Company' and 'The River'

The Tollesbury and Mersea Native Oyster Fishery Co. – 'The Company' as it was known in Mersea, or 'The River' as it was referred to at Tollesbury – began its operations in 1878 under the chairmanship of Dr. Hugh Green, of Strood Villa, West Mersea. Little is remembered of him, beyond the fact that he could not get on with his fellow director, Dr Salter. They are reputed to have met one day on the Peldon Road and settled their differences with a fist fight.[1] But despite his apparently low profile, he played an active role, being given funds and powers to purchase brood, and sometimes lending his own money for the purpose, for while the T. & M., unlike the Colne Company, had some capital it was not enough in the early days to make it self-financing. Nor did the finest nursery grounds in the country make it self-sufficient.

The capital comprised 3,000 £5 'A' shares, which were fully paid up and 3,000 £5 'B' shares reserved for the dredgermen of Tollesbury, East and West Mersea, Salcott and Bradwell, the designation of the two types of share having been reversed since the original proposals. Only 1,815 of the 'B' shares were, however, at the start paid up to £2 each, with a number of these in arrears.

The Articles of Association declared that profits were to be devoted firstly to a fund for members' widows and children, and secondly the payment of dividends. The former, reflecting a similar concern on the part of the Colchester and Whitstable Companies, which maintained a profit share for widows, was interpreted by allowing up to around £50 a year.

The latter aim was achieved only spasmodically, for the T. & M. was never to sustain the steady and substantial profitability of the Colne Fishery. By and large, up to the setbacks of the 1920s, the Colne made profits averaging £2,000 to £4,000 a year on gross sales from £10,000 to £20,000, with only eight losses between 1889 and 1930, while the T. & M. over the same period passed its dividend as often as it paid it, with turnover usually between £2,000 and £10,000, and overall losing nearly £10,000 on its first 40 years' operations. From the 1930s till the collapse in 1962, the T. & M. often did better than the Colne, but this was largely due to revenue from ships laid up on the Company's grounds, a windfall discussed later.

The Company also pledged itself to sell 'a sufficient quantity of young oysters (not spat) to stock the private layings contiguous' and to grant trawling licences to fishermen from places including Maldon, Heybridge and Goldhanger. The latter provision was, however, struck out before the

Company even started its operations, resulting in a bitter battle with the Maldoners which dominated its early years.

Directors appointed to represent the 'A' shareholders included John Smith of Burnham (who offered his *Helen* as a watchboat), and there were three directors each for Tollesbury and Mersea for the 'B' shareholders. For day-to-day management a jury was elected, along with two foremen, one each for Tollesbury and Mersea. General management was entrusted to a Water Bailiff. The wage for dredgermen employed on cleaning the grounds was fixed at 18 shillings a week (soon afterwards reduced to 16 shillings, then raised to £1 but down to 15 shillings in 1898) plus a shilling for working an extra dredge with wire ground but no net. Members of the jury received 2 shillings extra and the foremen 4 shillings. The Water Bailiff (W.A. Cooke) received 30 shillings a week, and the two watchmen £1 a week. The jurymen also had the privilege of continuous employment, which provoked a protest at the first annual meeting in 1880, after which it was ruled there should be only one juryman in each boat. Until 1886 the foremen worked afloat, but it was then decided to employ them 'on the marsh', leaving control of the boats to the jurymen in turn. The jury were also ordered to take their turn 'on the marsh', having apparently again tried to secure for themselves the privilege of full employment.

The working day was six a.m. to three p.m. (twelve noon on Saturday) and it was ruled that smacks of under ten tons might carry two men; those of ten to twenty tons two men and a lad; those of twelve to fifteen tons three men, and those of over fifteen tons four men. As in the case of the Colne Co. the number of boats to be set on each fortnight was decided according to seasonal needs and the state of the grounds. In May 1880 it was decided to work twenty boats, twelve from Tollesbury and eight from Mersea. This numerical preponderance was usually observed; indeed it is quite surprising that equal representation was accepted on the Board, for the rivalry between the two places was never far below the surface, though it never emerged as openly as the feuding of the Corporation and Company members in the Colne.

Stint working was also introduced to keep down labour costs, the stint being set in 1884 at 7 shillings per hundred oysters caught. The Tollesbury men objected, and as they were not paid for bringing in half-ware they threw it overboard. The Board protested that the system 'gave general satisfaction in Mersea', despite the fact that the previous July sixteen Mersea smacks, along with three from Tollesbury, refused their turn to work. For shifting brood and half-ware, a rate of 6 shillings a bushel was fixed, with a stint of six bushels per man per week. A halfpenny was also paid for each oyster caught – perhaps to discourage throwing these overboard also.

Stints varied from place to place, to an extent which makes the system difficult to understand fully. In 1886 in Deeps and Thornfleet it was 400 per man per day, paid at a rate of 11s. 3d. per thousand or 4s. 6d. per 400, and in Thirslet it was 500 a day at 9 shillings per thousand. Yet, presumably elsewhere, a stint of 300 a day was rejected as impossible and with the foremen refusing all but marketable oysters the dredgermen actually struck work. George Brand of Mersea said 200 a day was as much as a man could get, 'not including roughs'. Isaac Pullen of Tollesbury advised two Mersea men not to make their stint, for if they did it would not be reduced. This reached the ears of the Board which sacked Pullen from the Tollesbury jury. But soon after this thirty boats were set on, with a stint of 200 per man per day at 2s. 6d. a hundred.

The age when wages had to be kept below £1 a week was also the age when capital could be borrowed at three per cent, but even so the freedom with which the Company spent money on everything from brood to lawyers' fees, and boldly invested in pits and packing sheds, contrasts markedly with their anxiety to save every penny on those employed on cleaning and cultivation. In 1885 even the foremen were stood off and the allowance paid to watchmen for picking up brood was cut from sixpence per hundred to fourpence in 1886. As one reads the meticulous minutes of the innumerable meetings held to plan each fortnight's work, it is difficult to believe the Company was established in the interests of the dredgermen and that they in theory held half its control. They were continually exhorted to put back their wages into share purchases to improve the Company's financial position, but in view of what they were paid it is not surprising most were slow to do so.

The petty-mindedness was not confined to financial matters; indeed the continual fault-finding and imposition of trivial penalties suggest the regime of a boarding school run by bossy prefects under a weak headmaster. Smacks were repeatedly suspended for a year for any sort of offence, or the unproven suspicion of one. Any allegation that a boy had received a man's wage led to 10 shillings being withheld till the member could provide documentary evidence that he was of age. The Mersea *Pink* was in trouble for infringing a regulation ruling that no smack should be wholly crewed by members of one family. (This would have been the Hewes family, one of whom, Lewis ('Pinkie') Hewes, bears her name to this day.) The Mussetts' *Ida* had wages withheld because her crew used cultacs of a wrong shape or size. Then (in 1888) despite the fact that Clark Mussett was the Mersea foreman, or perhaps because of it, the Board solemnly resolved to sell 'no oysters to any Mussett'!

Sales in the early years were largely to local merchants such as E.L. Cooke and W.J. Bean at Mersea, John Smith at Burnham and Harvey and Heath at Wivenhoe, but there were also regular shipments to Ostend, where the buyers were constantly complaining of 'ugly, rough and dirty oysters' – chiefly, it would seem, to get the price reduced. These consignments were sent by the Dover mail and boats from London, but in 1886 the Tollesbury smack *Express* took a freight, and soon after Captain Hewes of the *Pearl* made several voyages, receiving a £1 gratuity for his sixth and seventh. This was probably a twenty-two ton yawl built at Brightlingsea in

1867 and owned by Adam Chatterson at Tollesbury – an unusual rig suggesting a carrier or coasting smack.

Whether there had originally been any real intention to grant trawling licences, or whether this was a ploy to gain acceptance for the Company, is not clear, but from the start Maldon was frozen out, repaying tit-for-tat the long years when the upper river had been a Maldon reserve and what had now become the Company's exclusive grounds had been a free-for-all.

Despite the emphasis on saving labour and a resolution to limit wages to £50 a week, two boats were told off at the first meeting 'to watch the Maldoners day and night', in addition to the permanent watchmen. Prosecutions did not stop poaching; one case apparently reached the High Court but resulted in 'ignominious defeat', through the failure of the Latchingdon magistrates' clerk to include the word 'knowingly' in the summons. Mersea boats also offended; when the *Monitor, Spray, Wave* and *Sarah* were caught trawling, their owners declared they 'wanted to try the case'. But the Maldoners were always the chief trouble. The Water Bailiff, sailing alongside a Maldon smack, was threatened with a gun. Asked what he thought he was up to, the Maldoner replied that he had a licence to shoot wildfowl. 'Not such as us', was the Bailiff's reply.

Publication of the Company's bye-laws in 1881 produced an objection from the Mayor of Maldon, who protested that 'the Company does not supply employment for one tenth of the persons who found employment previous to the grant', and complained that 'frequent criminal charges are injurious to the character of the Company and demoralising to the accused'. In the Crouch, he added, trawling was encouraged. Coldly, the Company invited him to supply exact figures of employment before and after the grant. For its part, the Company was frustrated to find its authority did not extend to prosecution under the Larceny Act, which carried a three-month prison sentence, but only to the limited powers conferred by the Sea Fisheries Act.

One of the quaintest priorities of the founders of the Company was their concern to provide poodle dogs for the watchmen. The Water Bailiff was told to look out for them and at first reported he could not find any, but he must in the end have succeeded, for payments approved in 1880 included one for dog biscuits. Apart from a poodle, the necessities of life provided by the Company were 'a bull's-eye, a spy-glass and a timepiece'. The watchman in the *Brazillia* used too much coal and was reprimanded.

On a more serious level the Company set to work in a purposeful way. Early spatfalls were not encouraging and the river was 'pocky and rossy'. But after obtaining a loan of £5,000 and advertising for 5,000 bushels of culch 'from the Nore, free from stone and large shells at 6d a bushel, delivered on Old Hall saltings', the Board in 1882 ordered 100,000 French oysters at 3 shillings per hundred, delivered direct by steamer, and laid half in Thirslet Creek (to please the Tollesbury element) and half in Deeps (to satisfy the Mersea men). The following year these had recouped the out-lay, with a good spatfall as well, and by 1890 all loans had been paid off.

The Mersea Packing Marsh Island was leased at £5 a year from H. May and a tender accepted to build the shed which still stands there, seventy feet by twenty-four feet, for the modest price of £48, though it does not seem to have been finished till 1887. Pits were dug by James Edwards and the Tollesbury smacks *Ripple, Village Maid, Pearl* and *Rosetta* brought culch for them, earning over £30 at sixpence a bushel. It was noted that 'to shell the remaining six pits 600 bushels will be needed, in addition to 140 bushels of stone'. Before enough pits were dug the stock had to take its chance in winter; in October 1881 nine boats were set on for a fortnight to take the oysters to pits and to lay brood and ware 'above Peldon Bar', the shoal ridge opposite the present Seaview Avenue, so called because it was located by a transit on Peldon Church.

Tollesbury Old Hall Saltings were hired from H. Cocks, of Guisnes Court, at £10 a year, and thirteen pits were dug there in 1886. These were followed next year by eleven more, each seventy feet by twenty-four feet, two feet deep at one end and two-and-a-half feet at the other, served by a canal 280 feet long, three-and-a-half feet deep and ten feet wide at the top. The remains of this considerable work, which cost £51, may still be seen. It was also decided to order a packing shed, to be built by Wyatt, but if this was ever built it has left no trace or further record. There seems to have been no thought of employing Company members on digging, which was again done on contract by Edwards.

Pilfering continued a problem. Several dredges were found with warps cut, usually a sign they had been abandoned for no honest reason, and also suggesting that the Company must have laid grapnels to catch them, no doubt on the Maldon frontier. Watchmen's wages were reduced in 1883 to 19 shillings on the upper grounds but left at £1 on the lower. The five watch boats evidently did not then always lie at anchor, as sails were bought for them, and in 1884 the *Native* was detected in Bradwell, with three watchmen ashore, an offence that cost each a fine of 2s. 6d. But, like the Colne Co., the T. & M. now found watchmen were not enough, and in 1883 applied to the Board of Trade for a warrant for Special Constables, 'as for Inspector Roance at Burnham'. This was refused. The Customs refused them powers to board vessels other than their own and the Chief Constable of Essex also proved unhelpful. Finally in 1888 the Company secured an agreement for the appointment of a sergeant and three constables, placing Sergeant Fletcher and one constable at Mersea and the other two constables at Tollesbury. Unlike the Colchester River Police, these were Special Constables, with the Company paying five per cent of their wages and finding their uniforms. As four watchmen were sacked it was a good bargain, even though a constable in 1887 received £70 12s., rising to £79 14s. after eight years including £5 for clothes, £1 6s. for boots and 12 shillings for oil for his bull's-eye. The police had a boat but may also have worked with the watch boats, of which there were now five, *Dauntless, Gleam, Native,*

Brazillia and *Betsey*. As well as outside poachers, the Company met indiscipline among its own members. The chairman's report for 1888 referred to 'a spirit of defiance' and warned that if orders were not obeyed 'the cash box will be locked up'.

These early years must have tested the Board's faith and nerve, as they invested thousands of pounds in stock and cleaning and sold only a few hundred pounds worth of oysters a year, swallowing up the working capital and leaving them faced with an indebtedness first to some of the directors (including John Smith who supplied £3,000-worth of oysters on six-month credit) and then to the bank. The report for 1883 solicited shareholders' patience, with assurances of ultimate success. Two years later Hugh Green felt the company 'warranted the employment of a capable, practical resident manager' and stressed the importance of finding a good market. Though by the following year half the outstanding loans had been cleared and, with sales reaching £12,748, a dividend was paid, neither of these aims seems to have been achieved.

Whether the Company would have fared better with more professional, dedicated management is a question which often suggests itself as one pursues its chequered fortunes. Despite periodical claims (often, as in 1893, to excuse a bad year's trading) that 'the highest prices in the market' had been secured, there is little evidence of any positive or consistent marketing policy. The Blackwater had been a feeder ground for Kent since before the time of the T. & M., for back in 1864-5 it exported 2,842 wash to Whitstable to the value of £11,676. Perhaps this was always its natural destiny, but the Company was still seeking to establish its independent self-sufficiency as late as 1915 when it opened its own depot at Billingsgate, though after the First World War it accepted an almost complete domination of its market by the Whitstable companies. A professional manager might have made the Blackwater as prosperous as the Colne, but more probably he would have found natural conditions insuperable, for time and again the oysters were green or ill-fished. Edward Stammers thought the Blackwater definitely superior to the Colne; he may have been right as to its capacity to produce brood, but it was never able to sustain the regular supply of first-rate white oysters on which success in the end depended. In any case Hugh Green's vision in practice never stood a chance, for he and his fellow directors did not have the power enjoyed by Colchester Corporation in the Colne to overcome the dredgermen's prejudice. His proposal to appoint a non-'B' shareholder was met with an amendment to include 'B' shareholders, and so check-mated.

Spatfalls were mainly poor during the 1880s, with increasing foreign competition. With no tradition of cultivation it took several years to discover the qualities of the various parts of the estuary; in 1887 the best fished oysters came from Deeps, but these tended to be green-finned, while those from outside were 'white, but not so well fished, and with pockey shells'. The following year it was decided that Deeps, the South Shore and the

Nass End were the best stock beds, with the two latter preferred for white oysters.

There was some recovery in 1890, with sales up to £15,735, the oysters better fished and more spat; in 1891, when sales reached £28,569, due to high prices; and in 1892 with sales of £21,470 and a profit of £1,676. A dividend was paid in this year, and again in 1893, despite a loss of £1,417 and sales down to £10,029, only half the previous year's figure.

The next ten years were unprofitable, with sales only once exceeding £10,000, in 1897 when the idea of a permanent foreman was discussed. The two years before this sales were affected by competition from Kent and by the poisoning 'scare'. Greening also continued a problem, and in 1898 £5,375 had to be spent on six million brood and half-ware to sustain stock.

There was another recovery in 1900, with a profit of £1,320 on sales of £8,130, rising to £9,045 in 1901 and £10,857 in 1902, despite lower prices and a renewed 'oyster scare', which reduced sales to £4,583 in 1903. Higher prices (again claimed as 'the highest on the market') made a slight improvement the next year, but the competition was too strong, and in 1905 there was a loss of £3,114 with sales shrinking to £2,033.

In that year the Company had to consider proposals from two railway companies to build piers on its grounds. The Great Eastern's Tollesbury pier was not opposed in principle and was in fact built. The first steamer departed from it for Clacton in September 1907, but it was not followed by many others, and the pier remained a white elephant till it was breached as a defence precaution during World War II and dismantled a few years later. A yet odder notion was the projected Colchester to Southend Light Railway, whose sponsors obtained Parliamentary approval for a pier at Bradwell to be linked by a steam ferry with another pier at West Mersea to connect with a railway station to be built on the Fairhaven Estate. This strange scheme never got beyond the realms of speculation, in both senses of that word.

The fishery now once again showed signs of recovery, making a profit in 1907 and paying dividends in 1908 and 1909, only to revert to losses up to the outbreak of war. During these years a change was made in the appointment of the jury, which up to 1911 consisted of a dozen dredgermen elected by the 'B' shareholders. The directors now insisted that these shareholders should select twenty-four candidates, from whom they could pick twelve. They also obtained the right to re-appoint foremen, who up to this time served for only one year, and at the same time moved the office from Colchester to Tollesbury. A motor launch was purchased in 1909, 'for dredging in fleet water and calms', followed in 1913 by the acquisition of the smack *Our Boys,* which was to serve the Company till its final working days. (She was ultimately sold in 1986.)

The outbreak of war rather surprisingly saw a return to profitability, with dividends annually from 1914 to 1920, with the exception of 1915 in which year the Billingsgate depot, already mentioned, was opened. Of more immediate importance, however, was a new emphasis on the sale of brood, which transformed the Company's finances. Sales of oysters continued at between £2,000 and £3,000 from 1917 to 1919, but a new sales figure for brood and half-ware then appeared, amounting to no less than £6,407 in 1917, £9,942 in 1918 and £2,286 in 1919. This was presented as a new departure, though there must have been receipts from this source earlier. On the debit side, slipper limpets proved an increasing problem, with the first loads going to the Mersea crushing station in 1916, and the following year there was a serious mortality on the South Shore.

The new policy reached its peak of success in 1920, with sales of oysters reaching £6,069 and brood £8,459, resulting in a profit of £5,119 – one of the few years when the T. & M. made a bigger profit than the Colne, which yielded £4,229 on a sales turnover of £17,231. The same year, the fearful mortality struck the fishery with the inevitable cruelty of a Greek tragedy. The record profit plunged to a loss of £3,307. Accounts showed that from its start in 1878 up to 1920 the Company's expenditure had exceeded its income by £9,495. The solution adopted in 1924 was a capital reconstruction, which permitted profits to be returned from 1924 to 1927, with a dividend in the two latter years, and again in 1929.

The 1930s brought poor spatfalls and low demand, with a damaging winter in 1931. The general depression, however, proved the Company's salvation, for a new source of revenue was found from ships laid up in the Blackwater. This checked the losses and in 1933 even produced a modest profit, with payments for shipping bringing in £1,620 and sales of oysters at £3,002.

Revenue from shipping was always described as 'compensation', for the simple reason that the Company's right to it under the terms of its Several Order was highly questionable. It was in fact questioned when the old Mersea herring fishery was established soon after the Second World War. [2] The ships anchored all over the estuary obstructed drift netting and it was proposed by the Kent and Essex Sea Fisheries Committee that they should be moored together in pairs or groups. The Ministry of Agriculture and Fisheries went further with a Draconian ruling that the ships should be removed entirely, but after some heated argument the Commissioners of Crown Lands intervened to claim their landlord's right, continuing the practice but demanding sixty per cent of the revenue and leaving only forty per cent for the T. & M., an arrangement which continues to the present day. It will be noted that once the lawyers took over the plea of the herring fishermen was forgotten and they got nothing.

Revenue from selling brood does not re-appear after 1920, but in 1935, when revenue from ships had temporarily declined, a new income was found from re-laying Brittany oysters for the Seasalter and Ham Co. This produced profits of £1,142 and £1,425 in 1936 and 1937, reducing the overall losses to £1,107 and £1,475. The two following years actually showed a profit. In 1938 natives brought in £4,610, and Brittanies a commission of

£1,693. In addition the Seasalter Co. contributed £1,362 for catching them towards a total wages bill of £3,321, giving the T. & M. a profit of £2,750. The same procedure yielded a small profit in 1939, but in 1940 easterly gales resulted in a disastrous mortality, with thousands of oysters smothered in silt on the South Shore and thousands washed up on the Mersea foreshore. This and the outbreak of war ended the project.

The war years, however, restored revenue from laid-up shipping and a regular profitability, with dividends paid in 1946 and 1947 and again in 1953 after an upturn in the sale of natives. After 1954 spat failed and sales flagged, till laid-up ships again reappeared. In 1959 revenue from this source (£3,396) exceeded the sale of oysters and the following year it amounted to no less than £8,448, yielding a 10 shilling dividend in both years, the profit in 1959 reaching £7,331.

In 1960, while sales of oysters yielded only £1,166 against revenue from shipping of £7,978, spatfalls had begun again and there was more brood than for some time. Within two years, Nemesis yet again took the hint and the opportunity to strike, with the winter disaster of 1962/63 which effectively ended serious oyster cultivation in the Blackwater.

Mersea in living memory

The story of the Mersea creek layings may conveniently be resumed at the time when they were coping with the slipper limpet plague and the intermittent mortality which in the 1920s was affecting cultivation all over Essex.

The limpets gave rise to a little local industry which demonstrates the scale of the infestation. A Dr. Jameson, who during the First World War came to live at the Firs, erected a crushing mill in his garden, which then extended to Firs Chase, and set up the Mersea Shell Crushing Co. to market the broken shell for chicken grit. A lighter was moored off Old Hall Point, in Mersea Quarters, and into this the smacks were expected to dump their limpets. According to Leslie French: 'Dr. Jameson was employed by the Government and wielded tremendous power . . . He was always sure of getting his required supplies of limpets because every fisherman had to hold a permit to work on the water. Dr. Jameson issued the permits and if anyone did not toe the line they ran the risk of having their permits withdrawn'.[1] When the lighter was full it was towed on to the Hard by an old smack named *Sela* and the limpets were taken up Firs Chase in tumbrils. The *Sela* also brought some loads from Burnham and, as has been mentioned, many tons came from the Colne. Modest payments were made for these supplies; possibly the T. & M. Co. received something for filling the Mersea lighter, but the dredgermen themselves had to accept it as just another chore.

In 1920 the Company built a new works at the head of the Ray Creek using a more sophisticated crushing and grading machine and leaving the huge old crushing stone where it lay as the garden of the Firs was converted into a housing estate around it. After about four years the new works was no longer profitable and was converted into the Shell Bungalow, Peldon, now the home and boatyard of John Milgate.

In the mud berths where smack yachts today are laid up in winter and fitted out in Spring may still be found the last traces of a smack, presumably the *Sela,* and the lighters she used to tow.

Despite the continuing mortality and relentless inroads of the limpets, a big spatfall around 1930, perhaps the result of the huge imports of Brittanies by the T. & M. Co. already mentioned, brought hopes of recovery, but they were short-lived and indeed the Company's own investment was destroyed a few years later by a series of easterly gales, which buried the oysters on the south shore under mud and sand and washed ashore those laid on the north side of the river.

Thus in the early 1930s most of the Mersea merchants were turning to

'Ports' to keep their layings in existence and themselves in business, though never to the total exclusion of natives, as had occurred at Brightlingsea.

The trade was on a big scale and involved a great deal of gruelling work. Up to half a dozen lorries, each carrying fifteen to twenty tons of seed oysters, would unload on the Hard, leaving a mountain of baskets, which in the 1930s had to be disposed of by skiffs and little sailing bumkins. The task took up to a fortnight, and grew daily more arduous as the baskets became sodden and heavy with accumulated mud. Working up to the grounds in the Strood Channel was straightforward, but the little voyage round to the other layings in Tollesbury Creek, deep-laden in all weathers, could be a taxing task.

By a happy chance one of these bumkins, George Stoker's *Boy George*, was in 1986 and 1987 entirely rebuilt in her original form as an evening-class project supervised by John Milgate at the Shell Bungalow, and should for many years remain as a living example of these brave little craft and the part they played in this phase of oyster cultivation.[2]

Cultivation was also laborious because the 'Ports' grew in clusters, which could not be parted and singled when they were small. The grower was thus faced with great clumps of heavy oysters, which had to be broken apart with the cultac, a thankless job which continued hour after hour with the huge quantities handled.

In addition to George Stoker, the chief Mersea cultivators were Ted Woolf, who employed up to eight men and had the biggest turnover of all, and Banks Brothers.

Fred and Henry (Harry) Banks began work together as fishermen, with their smack *Neptune,* in 1898, and went into oysters around 1900, with layings in the Strood Channel, opposite the Nothe, which they bought from the May estate in 1913, and some round in Salcott Creek. They were succeeded by Henry's sons, Jim and Harry. American oysters were also re-laid by them till about 1920, but thereafter their concentration was on 'Ports'.

By the 1930s there was intense competition, based largely on price, with Brightlingsea, which suffered the disadvantage of having to use a cleansing process described in Chapter 10. Moreover, the London merchants in the Brightlingsea trade sent their consignments to Billingsgate, while Banks supplied direct, visiting every seaside resort with a shellfish stall or restaurant, from Scarborough and Skegness, Margate and Ramsgate, Hastings and Paignton, to Tenby and Saundersfoot. Consignments were mostly sent by rail, which offered concessionary rates, and in 1936 the price was as low as 4s. 6d. a hundred delivered. The turnover was considerable, with a two-ton lorry-load going to Southend each week in the summer season. Banks Brothers bought for other Mersea merchants and also for Leslie's of Southend and on one occasion shipped a deck cargo of two **hundred tons into London docks, all in baskets, which the dockers charac-**teristically refused to unload due to some dispute, till a plea that they were

endangered livestock secured their release.

Supplies from Portugal, or sometimes Arachon in France, were received in February, because the import duty on oysters was suspended in favour of seed oysters during the winter months. Up to around 1950 small 40-gram oysters were bought, only about an inch long. When they were laid in the bed of a creek, they would establish themselves so firmly that a harrow had to be used to knock them loose and avoid the formation of hills. Their growth was so rapid that up to half were fit for sale during the summer, with the remainder kept for next year. Banks left theirs on the layings over the winter, risking damage from frost in order to avoid disturbing them, but some other cultivators used their pits. In the 1950s, however, the Tagus River stock became diseased and exports were banned by the Portuguese government. New supplies were found from the Sado Basin, but these did not grow at such a phenomenal rate, so larger oysters, of 60 to 100 grams, were preferred. These could be sold within a few months of re-laying; indeed some of the 'seed' oysters were found fit for market on arrival.

The trade reached its peak in the 1930s, when a Portuguese merchant, Senhor Santos, invited Fred Banks to visit him and, as a result of what he learned, hired many of the Mersea layings, for which there was then little demand. How many 'Ports' he shipped in is not reported, though estimates range from two to three million and the mountains of baskets are remembered to this day. Within two or three years the market was glutted, and many of the layings were smothered, and some permanently spoiled, by the huge abandoned shells, for the 'Ports' continued to grow till they were up to a foot in length, when they were unsaleable till during the latter years of the trade a Scarborough buyer was found who would take them.

The delicate new shell growth of native oysters was always tenderly protected, but as the 'Ports' began to outgrow their useful size they were sometimes thrown about with a heavel in order to knock it off. The overgrown monsters were laid at high water mark to die and their shells were used for making up edges. If they were allowed to die on the edges they accumulated mud and left hard lumps, which prevented the edge being raked flat and level. At this time of plenty, even Essex dredgermen, who seldom sampled a native, developed a taste for a few 'Ports' deep-fried in batter, and the steak and kidney pudding which was a tradition at the annual dinner of the Colchester Industries Association was judged by the number of oysters in each helping.

Banks Brothers' stocks were almost entirely destroyed in the catastrophe of 1962, and the loss, put at £32,000, might have ended the firm, but for a lucky chance. Pits full of natives somehow escaped and as a result of the scarcity their value rose six-fold. From the sale of these Harry Banks made a new start, benefiting from the ending of the Brightlingsea trade, till imports from Portugal were ended in 1976. He then tried Gigas, but found they did not grow on his layings, probably due to the effects of toxic anti-fouling paint and farmers' chemicals in the Strood Channel. He then reluctantly had to sow his grounds with the only profitable harvest left – yacht moorings.

Meanwhile the traditional native oyster trade gave some encouragement with renewed spatfalls in 1937 and 1938, only for recovery to be retarded by the war years and finally dashed again by the disastrous winter of 1945, which decimated stocks everywhere. Peter French has vivid memories of that sad aftermath, as the dredges brought up black heaps of the big 'Ports', the dead meat running out of them, mingled with the remains of the precious young natives.

New problems came in the 1950s when a fatal case of typhoid made the use of purifying plants compulsory. The Mersea men's response showed their traditional individualism. In any other trade, and at most other places, a shared project would have resulted, as at Brightlingsea, but at Mersea no-one's oysters must meet anyone else's oysters; if not actually contaminated they might be counted. So to this day five separate plants line the Coast Road between the present Victory Inn and its old predecessor at the bottom of The Lane, belonging to Banks Bros., Mussett, Woolf, the T. & M. Co. and Peter French.

Despite these setbacks and difficulties, the surviving cultivators continued to spend their savings on brood, encouraged by intermittent spatfalls, till by 1960 the Mersea layings were again almost self-sufficient, following a good spatfall on the Maldon grounds, which brought the price of brood down to 2 shillings a hundred.

Then came the catastrophes already described. The 1962/3 winter caused the destruction of almost every oyster in shallow water and most of those left in creeks hitherto believed to be deep enough for safety, though Peter French, like Harry Banks, found rather to his surprise that he had a few survivors in his wintering pits. On this occasion his memories are not so much of the almost total extinction of the native oyster stocks – that realisation came gradually – as of the damage to the grounds themselves, with the dredge having to clear away great lumps of 'cant' mud, pieces of the saltings which had been frozen into the ice and torn away as it melted.

He recalls, too, the subsequent efforts to make good the losses, and in particular his happy dealings with the Cornishmen, starting in 1963 and continuing for twenty years. Once age-old suspicions were overcome, some lasting friendships were established, commemorated in the naming of Peter's present Mersea home, 'Restronguet'. The trade was entirely by word of mouth and mutual trust, with the oysters all sold by number, not weight, and counted out by hand. As Peter's orders ran up to 30 tons,

Hauling and emptying oyster dredges on board the motor skiff Peewit.

141

averaging 15 to 20 thousand a ton, the counting gave both parties plenty of time to get to know each other.

He also engaged in the onslaught on the Stanswood Bay grounds in the Solent in 1971 when he was fishing out of North Shields in one of the *Mersea Lass*'s successors, *Providence*. Fitting her out with gigantic six-foot dredges, made for him by Taylors, the Abberton iron fabricators, and increasing his crew to five, he had anything but a warm welcome, but the voyage was a huge success and filled his grounds to overflowing. Several more such voyages to the Solent followed, though never with the same success, especially after the best grounds were closed by a Several order.

The last of the thousand-year-old Mersea layings had begun to disappear following the winter of 1963, and few were left to face the final blow twenty years later, a period during which there was never an appreciable spatfall. Yacht moorings were found more profitable than culch and brood on the bed of Mersea Fleet beside the now abandoned packing shed and in the Buzzen, so long the Mussetts' preserve. In the Strood Channel they spread upwards, from Hempstead's ground opposite the old Victory over Banks Bros' and Robert Stoker's pieces to the layings so stoutly defended by Cassell French, where a new yacht centre has developed with its own causeway to the caravan park, though Peter French continues a little cultivation there to this day. He has learned, however, to prefer his grounds in Tollesbury Creek, which are further from interference by pleasure craft, and in particular from pollution by the toxic anti-fouling paints applied to their bottoms. Finally in 1986 the Mersea waterfront lost its most charming feature with the closure of the roadside oysterage, created by Ted Woolf, a perfect little microcosm of the vanishing oyster world, with its little timber and tile packing shed, its quay and boat dock and its pits neatly cut in a patch of ground carefully made up and protected by wooden walls.

Yet Salcott Creek, apart from the lowest reach, 'Doitch' (the old Little Ditch') and much of Tollesbury Creek remain inviolate, even if in many places neglected and fouled with mud. To date the industry is just surviving in these areas by the relaying of a few tons of oysters from the Solent area in hopes that these amounts may be increased if the Bonamia does not remain as virulent as when it first struck.

Survivals and revivals

The ravages of Bonamia, compounded by the poisoning from farmers' weed-killers and T.B.T. anti-fouling paint, were the final blow to traditional oyster cultivation, already weakened by the disaster of the 1962-63 winter, which had reduced stocks below the levels necessary for survival and revival, at a time when traditional sources for replacement had largely disappeared.

The Colne lay abandoned for two years as Colchester Corporation looked round for a tenant to replace the defunct Colne Fishery Company. An offer from Mrs. Marie Mussett of West Mersea, backed by the directorship of the Savoy Hotel, was accepted, but proved abortive. Then in 1965 a 42-year lease was granted to Christopher Kerrison, a former racing-car driver with a deep love of the Essex estuaries which he knew as a wildfowler.

Aided by the last Company foreman, Jack Francis, who never lost faith in the possibilities of revival, Mr. Kerrison's Colchester Oyster Fishery Ltd tackled an uphill task with vigour. Though his first year sales were a mere 3,000 oysters he set about re-stocking with natives from Cornwall and the Solent, as well as American Gigas oysters as a stop gap. Nature gave little support; a spatfall in 1967 was the first seen for five years, but it had little lasting effect. The expenditure of £20,000 on Cornish stock in 1971, however, made profitable trading a possibility for the first time, with the Colne now the third largest fishery in the country, the two others being in Cornwall.

It soon became apparent that Peewit Island was hopelessly obsolete as a headquarters and for a few years operations were conducted from premises on the shipyard site at Brightlingsea, but planning restrictions and the development of a dock scheme rendered this untenable and the bold decision was taken in 1978 to build a new oysterage at North Farm, East Mersea, with modern handling equipment and a new access to Pyefleet. This handsome building, resembling many of the oysterages on the marshes of Western France, represented the biggest venture in Essex oyster cultivation since the building of the old packing sheds in Pyefleet and at Mersea nearly a century before.

The act of faith was justified by an agreement in 1975 with the Loch Ryan Fishery in Wigtownshire, one of the finest natural spatting grounds in Europe, which had been spared the effects of the 1962-3 disaster thanks to the protection of the Gulf Stream, which washes the west coast of Scotland. The Loch Ryan Oyster Fishery Co. Ltd. was set up in 1901, based on a 200-year-old charter. Though before the First World War millions of oysters, from Whitstable, France and Cornwall, as well as its own local 'Loch Ryans', were laid on its grounds inside the Scaur, its isolation seems to have preserved it from many of the pests debilitating the heavily worked Essex fisheries. Natural spat here was augmented from a hatchery in the Isle of Lewis.

With these resources behind it, the Colne at last seemed once again to have real prospects, and an ingenious dredging machine was built to make the most of them. A catamaran with a platform deck even more ample than that of the old Pyefleet paddler, it hauled its heavy dredges hydraulically, a system devised by an expert in this field, Ian Young, of P.N.P. Duerr at Burnham. It could also lift trays (then favoured as a likely form of cultivation) on deck between its hulls without affecting its stability. It was built not in a shipyard but by Taylor's, the Abberton metal fabricators, and the best comment on its peculiar ugliness is that it must have been the only oyster dredger built which did not even acquire a name. Hydraulic winches on the Company's more conventional motor skiff also enabled dredges to be hauled in pairs, slung from a frame.

These far-seeing policies received a setback when Bonamia reached the Colne in 1982. All stock was cleared from Pyefleet to allow a three-year period of disinfection, and, while some supplies continued to be received from Loch Ryan, the fishery resorted to diversification into the handling of lobsters, clams and other seafood, as well as the development of its tourist potential by attracting parties of visitors. Whether – or when – nature will one day relent and allow the seeds sown with such faith and courage to bear fruit in the form of a real revival of the Pyefleet's old glories is one of the more challenging questions facing the oyster trade today.

The grounds abandoned by the Roach River Co. in 1963 attracted the interest of the Ministry of Agriculture and Fisheries, which was undertaking considerable research and experiment into the restoration of native oyster fisheries. Its laboratory at Burnham made extensive water samplings, intended to advise cultivators when to expect a spatfall and lay culch. A 'diving dredge' was also produced, but neither innovation obtained wide acceptance and after a few years the shellfish research was transferred to Lowestoft, though work on pollution continues at Burnham.

Using the research boat *Wystris*, the Ministry surveyed the old River Roach Co. grounds in 1965, finding a sprinkling of surviving oysters, all on the north side of the river. Whitehouse Hole, a noted spatting ground, still had clean culch, some good oysters and only a few limpets. A lease was granted to the Kent and Essex Sea Fisheries local district committee in 1967, with a recommendation to break the ground up into sixteen small layings, to secure intensive cultivation. The Roach River Co., granted 350 acres a century before, had never cultivated more than fifty.

Most of these plots were in 1976 and 1977 leased by a Mersea businessman, Norman Childs, who had no oystering background but who had a consuming passion for every aspect of the trade. Having disposed of his Mersea yacht agency, he looked around in 1976 for an opportunity to satisfy this enthusiasm, but, finding nothing available, decided instead to invest in a bakery in Sudbury. This was only a few weeks before he heard of the leases offered at Paglesham. Undaunted, he accepted the challenge of undertaking two new careers simultaneously and has continued for the past ten years to manage both concerns.

In that time the Roach has provided plenty of experiences and adventures for his Paglesham Oyster Co. As the Ministry survey had suggested, the northern side of the river above Paglesham Pool was soon restored to workable condition, using the old Tollesbury stowboater *My Alice,* yet the opposite side remained irretrievably smothered in slipper limpets.

Having cleaned some ground, the first problem was to stock it. Dealings with Cornish and Southampton suppliers left Norman Childs increasingly disillusioned by erratic deliveries and escalating prices, till he discovered a Cornish fishery which had been closed for a curious reason. The Lynher and Tamar grounds, on the Tamar River, under the Saltash railway bridge, and so one of the most beautiful oyster fisheries in the world, were in excellent condition, but had earned a bad reputation for causing sickness among consumers. No cause could be discovered, but around 1950 a purifying plant had been installed and a little oyster banquet held to celebrate it. But, alas, the old symptoms recurred among those taking part and the fishery was closed. Reflecting on this, Norman Childs concluded that the trouble must be some algae of purely local origin and was fortunate to find at the Ministry an officer prepared to agree that if they were re-laid in Essex waters for not less than three months the Tamar stock might be approved for consumption.

The former dredgermen, still disconsolately surveying their old livelihood, were delighted to take licences, prudently limited to the out-of-season months of April to June, to prevent disposal elsewhere, and with the aid of its own small boat, sent down by road, the Paglesham Co. re-laid twenty-five tons from this source in 1980. The transfers, which have continued year by year, are carefully supervised by Ministry order, with the bags having to be sealed at Saltash by a local health official and checked by a corresponding official of the Rochford District Council before being re-opened in Essex.

In addition to this enterprise, Norman Childs undertook two interesting ventures in artificial rearing. An eel importing company at Heybridge Basin used a steel floating tank, with a perforated bottom to allow water circulation, to store its eels, and when this concern closed down he acquired this and stocked it with a quarter of a million three-millimetre oyster spat from a hatchery, placed for safety in boxes and nets. The growth was good; in fact it was too good to handle, for after a few weeks the contents of a hundred boxes had to be transferred into two hundred, then after another few weeks into four hundred, till the whole process became too labour-intensive to be practicable, especially as the young brood proved to be too vulnerable to be laid in open water.

Norman Childs therefore turned to rearing in his Paglesham purifying plant, which comprises a number of small tanks instead of the large single tank used in most of the Mersea plants. These tanks were carefully cleaned, lined with black polythene and filled with water filtered through the finest possible screen. Culch of every sort, from oyster, cockle and mussel shell to chopped-up bits of plastic hose, was laid in perforated trays and the water was warmed to a temperature around seventy degrees Fahrenheit. Half a million eyed larvae from the Seasalter hatchery were put in, and settled after two hours. Three weeks later a worthwhile load of spat shell was taken to the pits and successfully grown on. Significantly, almost all of the successful spat fell on oyster shell, with some on mussels. Cockle shell yielded nothing; indeed in one tray of cockle shell an oyster shell had been dropped by accident and in that tray only this shell was fruitful.

It would be nice if that were the end, or better still the beginning, of the story, but, alas, when the experiment was tried again the following year it produced no result at all. The only difference Norman Childs can call to mind is that on the first occasion the water used happened to be covered with an unusually heavy outcrop of the seasonal summer growth known to fishermen as 'tobacco juice'. This is generally regarded with such disfavour that fishermen suspend operation when it appears, but could it produce some algae favourable for spatfall?

At present the Paglesham Oyster Co., like many others, is scaled down till the ravages of Bonamia, hopefully, pass. Paglesham village showed its appreciation at the revival of its traditional industry by starting an annual oyster festival which in the early 1980s grew into a highly popular event.

The most ambitious venture into artificial production was carried out by Peter French on his grounds in Tollesbury North Channel.

In the mid-1970s, when it was apparent that appreciable natural spatfalls could no longer be hoped for, and that supplies from the Fal and the Solent were becoming uneconomic and unlikely to meet a sustained demand, the Ministry of Agriculture and Fisheries were beginning to achieve some success with spatting under laboratory conditions at Conway, following years of experiment. This was achieved by suspending the spat from a few oysters in swirling water till they grew large enough to collect. One or two commercial hatcheries were set up, chiefly devoted to Gigas, which were comparatively easy to produce, but some native *ostrea edulis* were being offered, though without much response, due to the intensive care and high mortality rate over the four to five years needed to grow the small spat, two to ten millimetres in size, into marketable oysters.

The Ministry had also experimented by placing the seed spat in a stack of fine-mesh trays and pumping sea water upwards through them. Peter French adapted this system, placing the trays in a plywood box, with a scoop-shaped mouth at the bottom. This was anchored afloat in the creek so that the tide forced water up from the scoop through the trays and out at the back of the box. A tide rate of one to two knots was required.

These boxes the Ministry scientists christened 'flupsies'. The first few *Survivals and* produced some half-ware, but mortality was heavy and there were losses *revivals* from mishaps unforeseen through lack of experience. But the result was sufficiently encouraging to justify further development which, it was clear, had to be on a much larger scale to accommodate the equivalent of hundreds of 'flupsies' each containing ten trays. Peter's solution was to build a raft, sixteen feet square and four feet six inches deep, the size of twenty-four 'flupsies', thus accommodating 240 trays, some of which were brought from France purpose-made of plastic. The following year this brought moderate success, but again with a high mortality and unacceptable losses, many due to human error. The growth of the survivors was, however, phenomenal, with a ten-fold increase in a few weeks.

Three more rafts were built for the third year, with another much larger one ordered from a local steel works. As the rafts had to be anchored where they caught the full force of the tide, and to swing to catch both flood and ebb, mooring them securely was just one of the problems. Soon, however, three quarters of a million seed were keeping three men fully occupied, for every two weeks each stack of ten trays had to be taken out, hosed through to remove the silt, and the oysters sifted into various grades, using stainless steel sieves. If this was not done only about a quarter would grow, for it seemed that the larger oysters in each tray consumed most of the food and it was necessary to keep all the same size together.

Growth rates of one-and-a-half inches to two inches were obtained in one season from ten-millimetre seed. This created problems of space, for although the four rafts started with only ten per cent of the space occupied, soon every raft was full and other steps had to be taken. Plastic mesh bags were used for the larger brood of one inch and over, and were put on racks at low-water mark, following a practice of some French growers. These needed less attention, but ultimately the only solution was to lay the oysters on the layings when they reached a size of one-and-a-half inches, which it was hoped the crabs would find difficult to eat.

By 1983 two layings were stocked with hatchery-produced oysters – something no other commercial oyster farmer had been able to achieve. The next year it was planned to market considerable numbers and settle down to purchasing a million seed a year, which it was estimated three men could cope with. It had proved an exciting venture and Peter French's enthusiasm was fully shared by his two workmates. The native oyster has an intrinsic beauty of its own; when it is mature the shell has a lustrous gleam and the weight of the meat within makes it a pleasure to hold in the hand. The young brood are even more attractive, with their delicate fringe of pink-tinged shell showing the promise of growth to come. This unique nursery was thus more than a commercial enterprise; it charmed and fascinated the three men creating it.

And it was at this juncture that Bonamia struck. A few of the nursery oysters reached the market, but thousands died and thousands more had to be destroyed. It was a microcosm of the story of so much native oyster culture, with the fruits of faith, patience and dogged toil so often destroyed by unforeseen natural disasters.

It could all be tried again, though it would demand a heavy investment in money, faith and labour. The tragedy is that it probably never will be.

Glossary

Barr	Sea Urchin.
Beacon	Post or sapling driven into mud or saltings to mark boundary of laying, shoal ground etc. Occasionally a floating spar serving the same purpose.
Beard	The oyster's fins, or gills, the tissue around the plump meat. Also called mantle.
Blubber Weed	Seaweed also known as sea squirts or 'pissers'.
Brood	Young oysters.
Bumkin	Scoop-rigged open boat with short iron bowsprit giving the name.
Cant	The cliff-like edge of the saltings. Also the flats of the North Kent shore below the Medway.
Chapstick	Wooden bar spreading back of dredge rigging, used to lift and empty contents.
Clock	Pair of dead or dying oyster shells.
Cock	Oysterman's boat (Paglesham, 16th century).
Culch	Spat-collecting material, usually clean shell. (Laver insists that cultch is the correct spelling, perhaps to suggest a connection with cultivation, but in Suffolk cultch signifies rubbish or substandard stuff such as unpalatable food.)
Cultac	Blunt dagger-shaped knife for parting and singling oysters.
Docker	Wicker basket holding about 1½ to 2 bushels, but not one of the measures of size.
Docking	Shaking and washing mud from dredge or basket.
Dolly Legs	Wooden pieces on side of dredge rigging.
Dredge	Triangular iron frame, with hoeing edge or scythe (q.v.) and net to catch oysters. Also verb, hence dredgerman.
Dump	Small, thick, slow-grown oyster.
Dydal (Didall)	Net on long handle. (In Tusser's *Husbandry*, a triangular spade on long handle for cleaning ditches.)
Ebbing	Collecting oysters and brood exposed by low water.

Edge		The edge of a laying usually between low-water marks of neaps and spring tides, often made up with stone, chalk or shram for the laying of oysters.
Evil		See Heavel.
Edulis		*Ostrea edulis.* The true native oyster. The European flat oyster, acclaimed as the best, most succulent oyster – and the most expensive.
Fished		A fat oyster is called well fished.
Five-Fingers		Star fish.
Fleet		Creek or channel. Literally of little depth, shallow.
Flupsy		Nickname given by Ministry scientists to breeding boxes designed by the Ministry and modified by Peter French at Mersea.
Frail		Another name for an oyster basket.
German Writing		Cement-like deposit making scrawly pattern on oyster shell or stones.
Greening		Oysters produced in some Essex creeks and rivers had a noticeable green coloration in the beard (q.v.), unlike the creamy, sandy colour of those from the Colne and elsewhere. Buckland attributed the colour to the presence of a sea-weed known as crow-silk. They were much prized in Ostend and France, but not so popular in London, possibly because confused with Cornish oysters which took on a green tinge from minerals deriving from nearby mining areas.
Gigas		*Crassostrea gigas.* An oyster native to the Pacific, widely cultivated in Japan and Australia. It has been very successfully reared artificially in the U.K. where production is increasing rapidly.
Hale		Haul, often used up to the 18th century.
Haul-and-End		Method of dredging close-hauled against unfavourable wind, having only one haul then returning to cover the same patch again.
Haul-Tow		Dredging by hauling skiff up and down a laying. In Cornwall, Tow-Haul.
Heavel		Close-tined fork, usually pronounced evil, which may be correct as it was considered damaging to user's boots and feet. But spelled heavel in Tollesbury and Mersea Co. records.

Heel	The lug on the ring end of the dredge, used to lodge it on the smack's rail. Hence heel-to-tide, the way a dredge should be cast so that it will reach the ground in the correct position.
Hoove	Wooden drain for oyster pits.
Knubb	An ill-grown, deformed oyster.
Laying	An area of ground on which oysters are laid.
Ledgen	Small pit, or floating tank, usually used for storing consignments required for sale or other special purposes. Corrupted to 'Legend'.
Logging	Towing dredges in calm, or against light foul wind, by letting the tide carry the smack broadside.
Mantle	See Beard.
Metes	Beacons (q.v.). Two posts usually positioned on the saltings so that when in line, the transect leads across the creek at right angles to its flow and indicates the boundary between the oyster layings.
Overlanders	Burnham dredgermen who were ferried daily across the Crouch in overland boats to Overland Point, whence they walked along the sea wall to work at Paglesham.
Pit	Shallow artificial pond for oyster storage.
Pock	Small red growth on oyster shell.
Port	*Crassostrea angulata*. A Portuguese oyster originating in the River Tagus. Imported in large numbers between the Wars and after the Second World War. Production was decimated by pollution in the late sixties. No longer available, stocks having been virtually wiped out.
Prickle	Oyster measure. Laver suggests because originally made from brambles, which sounds improbable. In living memory mostly made of hedgerow elm. At Mersea and Paglesham, usually priddle.
Rigging	The bottom of the dredge bag, originally of hide, latterly of wire rings.
Ring	1. Measure used in some fisheries to determine minimum size of oysters to be caught, usually about two inches. No oyster which would pass through the ring might be kept.
	2. Wire circle used to make dredge riggings (q.v.) Hence 'ring-hide', Maldon name for rigging, curiously confusing old and new methods.

Ross	Sandy coraline growth inhabited by red worm. Food for shrimps, but a pest to oysters.
Scrail	A haul or series of hauls with smack hove-to.
Scythe	The hoeing edge of the dredge. In Cornwall a blade.
Several Order	Lease of ground under jurisdiction of Crown Commissioners.
Sheards	Pair of boards about eighteen inches by six inches, for gathering stuff from smacks' deck. Pronounced shards.
Short Tides	From the first day before the full moon, till high water was around 3 p.m., a short day was worked to enable sailing smacks to reach their moorings by high water.
Shram	Small broken shell used to make up edges (q.v.).
Shuts	Small rings joining rings of dredge rigging (q.v.).
Singling	Parting clusters of oysters or removing oysters from culch.
Skiff	Work boat, usually clinker built. Those for haul-tow (q.v.) were usually double-ended, but others, including the motor skiffs which displaced sailing bumkins, had transom sterns and were very beamy and flat-floored.
Skilling	Corruption of Terschelling, a deep-sea oyster fishery. Hence skillinger, deep-sea smack.
Slud-driver	Rake-like implement, but with flat blade instead of tines. Used to push mud off layings or stir up mud off beds so that tide will take mud away.
Spat	Oyster less than one year old. Also verb indicating spitting out by the fertile oyster.
Spat-shell	Culch shell with spat on it.
Splasher	Undershoe consisting of a piece of wood with two rope strops to slip over a sea boot. Used for walking on mud and to avoid leaving footprints on oyster grounds. At Tollesbury, a splatcher.
Stinting	Piece-work payment for dredging, according to the quantity or stint set.
Summer dredger	Dredgerman allowed to work in summer close season. Originally a charitable dispensation.
Tendil	Oval bowl-shaped basket made from hedgerow elm, with bow handle. From Dutch teen: osier, and teentje; small wicker basket.

Tingle	Boring shellfish which kills young oysters by injecting a poison.
Trug	A flat oyster basket.
Tub	Oyster measure. In 1822 a tub measure was approved at Burnham on Crouch as holding 94 quarts or 23½ gallons beer measure.
Ware	Immature oysters requiring one more year's growth. Half-ware, younger oysters.
Warp	The rope attached to the dredges and used to haul them in. Used to be made of coir (coconut fibre), very rough to the hand.
Wash	Oyster measure. In 1822 a wash measure was approved at Burnham on Crouch as holding 21 quarts, 1 pint.
Winkle Brig	Small fisherman's boat, usually lug rigged (West Mersea).
Withy	Sapling beacon (q.v.). Seldom used by oystermen who always referred to beacons.
Wolded	Rope or strands of rope wrapped around the scythe or hoeing edge of the dredge to make it less likely to dig deep into a muddy bottom.

Footnotes

Introduction

1 Horace Round, in *Victoria County History of Essex,* Vol 1 (1903) considers that the Essex Fisheries recorded in the Domesday Survey were probably fixed fish traps known as 'kettles' or 'kiddles'. Those on or near the coast were at Mistley, Little Oakley, Clacton, East Mersea (4), West Mersea, Tollesbury, Osea Island, Bradwell, Lawling, 'Hacfleet' (unidentified but in the Dengie Hundred), Tillingham, Southchurch (2), Benfleet, Vange, Fobbing, Horndon, Mucking, Tilbury, Chadwell, Grays Thurrock, West Thurrock, Barking and Ilford.

2 Murie, James: *Report on the sea fisheries and fishing industries of the Thames estuary* (1903).

3 Dr Murie of Leigh analysed the spatfalls from 1846 to 1900 as twelve very bad (1851-1864, except 1857, 1858, 1859), 26 moderate and 17 very good, especially 1849, 1859, 1876, 1881 and 1884, with 1893 and 1900 'quite remarkable'. Laver (ERO, Colchester Branch C133) noted 1897, 1902, 1903 fair, 1905 good, 1909 failure, 1910 poor, 1911 small. My summary of prices is from an article in the *Essex Standard,* 19 March 1885, quoted by Philpots, John: *Oysters and all about them* (1891) which is broadly in agreement.

4 Mayhew, Henry: *London labour and the London poor* (1864).

5 *Cholera in England in 1893.*

6 *Guardian,* 20 March 1987, quoting *Parasitology Today.*

7 Cole: *Oyster cultivation in Britain* (H.M.S.O., 1956).

8 Bulstrode states that in 1894 the East Coast produced 16,837,000 oysters to a value of £56,300; the South Coast 4,251,000 (£11,186) and the West Coast 6,630,000 (£14,780).

9 Evidence to the Select Committee on Oyster Fisheries, 1876.

10 Pollard, A. O.: *The oysters and dredgers of Whitstable* (1902).

11 Shenstone, J.C.: 'Oyster fisheries' in *Victoria County History of Essex,* Vol. 2 (1907).

Chapter 1

1 Peter French remembers seeing a skinback dredge hanging in the shed of Munson, the Mersea coal merchant.

2 Philpots, J.; *op. cit.* Mid-19th century diaries of the Wiseman family of Paglesham contain an address in Monument Street, London, where buffalo tides could be obtained for use in dredge bottoms.

3 Frank Cock of Restronguet.

4 In 1983 tidal erosion near the King's Hard at West Mersea revealed the remains of an old double-ended boat, which curiously was fastened with 'trenails' or wooden pegs, and still had unopened oyster shells in her bottom. The boat was recovered from the mud by John Milgate, the Peldon shipwright and carbondated by the National Maritime Museum.

Chapter 2

1 Public Record Office: Customs Letterbooks, Maldon.

2 Fuller, Thomas: *Worthies of England* (1622).

3 Dickin, Edward P.: *A history of the town of Brightlingsea: a member of the Cinque ports* (1913).

4 Colchester and Essex Museum collection.

5 The Seasalter and Ham Co. traded from Whitstable and were buyers of oysters from Essex which they relaid, for a season, on the Kentish flats. When sold they were Whitstable natives! They were in opposition to the older Whistable Co. and latterly operated on a bigger scale. They had grounds in the Crouch and Roach and were large shareholders in the Tollesbury and Mersea Oyster Co., on whose oysters they naturally had first call.

6 *Seasalter* (FM. 322) was built at Whitstable in 1875. She was 51.8 feet long, 14.2 beam, 7.8 hold depth, 29 reg. tons. She was also used for dredging on the Kentish flats, for which her size and heavy gear made her hard work, till she was broken up in 1936. Her skipper, Albert Stroud, was also a professional yachtsman, and was aboard the *Britannia* when she was scuttled after the death of King George V. When he returned to Whitstable and found the *Seasalter* in pieces he was heartbroken, and bitterly referred to 'the two greatest maritime crimes of the century' (See A. Stroud: 'Whitstable Oystermen' in *Bygone Kent*, Feb. and March 1987). *Speedwell*, built at Burnham in 1908 for Smith Bros. and registered by them as CR 314, is today a yacht at Shoreham.

Chapter 3

1 Sprat, Thos.: *History of the Royal Society* (1667).

2 Colchester Corporation v. Prestney and others, and Coveney and Hawkins v. Mayor, Aldermen and Burgesses of Colchester.

3 J. Horace Round, a giant among Essex historians, also took Dickin's view, attacking Morant's interpretation of the charter as an attempt to please the Corporation. See 'Lionel de Bradenham and Colchester': Essex Archaeological Society *Transactions*, Vol XIII (1910).

4 *Essex County Standard*, 25 June 1898.

5 The verbatim reports of the case, and of the appeal, each occupy two massive bound volumes, with another for the judgements, and over a dozen more devoted to instructions, pleadings, letters, transcripts and other matters. All are in the Essex Record Office. Pulleyne had to pay £2,700 in costs, yet on his death in 1913 he bequeathed his riverside rights to the Corporation – either to bury the hatchet or to show he still felt he had something to leave. Dickin, in his *History of Brightlingsea*, refers to a synopsis of deeds relating to the Manor of Brightlingsea by B. C. Pulleyne (privately printed).

6 Essex Record Office.

7 Dickin, *op. cit.*

8 Morant, Philip: *The history and antiquities of the town and borough of Colchester* (1748).

9 Bacon, Nathaniel: *Annals of Ipswich*, a 17th-century record of early documents, edited by W. H. Richardson (1884).

10 Clark, Rev. A.: 'Oyster dredging in 1675', *Essex Review*, Vol. XXI (1912).

11 Defoe, Daniel: *Tour through the whole island of Great Britain* (1724).

12 Leather, John: *The Northseamen: The fishermen, yachtsmen and shipbuilders of the Colne and Blackwater rivers* (1971).

Chapter 4

1 Abstract of leases, Essex Record Office.

2 See Benham, H.: *The Salvagers* (1980).

3 Rules and Regulations of Maldon Fishery, Essex Record Office.

4 Perhaps the great-grandfather (b.1781) of the last Colchester sailing barge owner, Joshua Francis (1876-1956). The Francis family lived in the 18th century at Heybridge Hall, and also at Ulting Hall and Stocks Hall, and over four generations named the eldest son Joshua (Essex Record Office).

5 See Benham, H. and Finch, R.: *The Big Barges* (1983).

6 See Benham, H.: *The Smugglers' Century* (1986).

7 Pennell, H.C.: *Report to the Board of Trade* (1870).

8 Colin Brookes of Heybridge: *Colchester Evening Gazette,* 18 Feb. 1986.

Chapter 5

1 Abstract of title, Crouch Fisheries, Essex Record Office.

2 The Mildmays settled at Moulsham, near Chelmsford, in the time of Henry VIII. Sir Thomas Mildmay married Lady Francis Ratcliff, half-sister of Thomas, Earl of Sussex, and heiress to the long line of Fitzwalters. Lord Fitzwalter was succeeded in the title by his brother, Benjamin Mildmay, who was raised to the rank of Earl, but as he died without issue in 1756, the title became extinct (*Essex Review,* V,185 and XX,171).

3 Norden, John: *Speculi Britanniae Pars: an historical and chorographical description of the county of Essex* (1594); ed. Sir Henry Ellis (1840).

4 For details see Benham, H.: *The Smugglers' Century* (1986). For Richmond's shipowning, including the famour ketch barge *Lucy Richmond,* see Benham, H. and Finch R.: *The Big Barges* (1983).

5 *Essex Standard,* 10 June 1882.

6 Shenstone, J. C., *op. cit.*

7 Crush v. Allen: Essex Record Office (which also contains a collection of leases filed as Peter Crush papers).

8 Letter to *Sunday Express,* 2 June 1974, from W. F. Stebbings, who claimed she was the last oyster dredger built by his grandfather, which on the evidence quoted seems not exactly correct.

9 The Chelmsford-published *Essex Almanac* starts in the 1870s to refer to the 'Crouch River Oyster Co.', but this seems to have been a local title of convenience to distinguish it from the Roach River Co., which saw its principal development at this time. Kelly remains faithful to 'Burnham Oyster Fishery Co. Ltd.'. As a further complication, E. Smith is reported in 1906 as the secretary to the River Roach Co. so it is possible that the whole realignment was more complex than I have suggested.

Chapter 6

1 Essex Record Office.

2 Undated estate map by Offin & Rumsey, Rochford. Survey by Royal Engineers, Shoebury, 1955. Survey by M.A.F.F. Burnham and Kent and Essex Sea Fisheries Committee, 1977.

3 Benham, H.: *The Smugglers' Century* (1986); Roberts, Rosemary: *Paglesham, life in an Essex marshland village* (privately published, 1972) to which I am indebted for much of the rest of this chapter.

4 *Jumbo* and *Alice* were a couple of elephants who captured public fancy in a way which is a reminder that silly news stories did not start with the mass media. Colchester's water tower, also a product of the 1880s, was christened Jumbo, the story being summed up in the jingle:

> Jumbo said to Alice 'I love you'.
> Alice said to Jumbo 'I don't believe you do,
> For if you loved me truly, as you say you do,
> You wouldn't go off to America and leave me in the Zoo'.

5 *Kate* was built at Paglesham by Hall, who was followed by Kemp, who was followed by Shuttlewood, father and son. The shed is now used by W. H. and L. G. Norris for fitting out fibre-glass hulls.

6 *Essex Standard*, 23 August 1867.

7 Pennel, H. C.: *Report to the Board of Trade* (1870).

8 Shenstone, J. C.: *op. cit.*

9 *Mistral* (Journal of the Mersea Island Society), winter 1981-2.

Chapter 7

1 Other ownerships noted include the following. Woolvett's son Joseph, a Brightlingsea innkeeper, in 1859 sold layings for £450 to Robert Francis of Brightlingsea. In 1866 these passed to Sir John Johnson, of St. Osyth's Priory, who sold to George Harvey of Wivenhoe for £700 in 1884. The sale comprised a laying of 16 perches in North Fleet; a laying 'sometime Oakley's' lying between a laying 'sometime of William Leaper' and layings 'formerly of Thomas Sach, and afterwards of William Flack'; the laying 'at the east extremity of North Fleet abandoned and restored by Samuel Woolvett'; and a laying 'at the east end of North Fleet formerly of Thomas Sach, later Charles Cox and then Robert Francis, Sen.'.

A deed of 1650 refers to a laying 'late of John Branch in Millfloot alias North Fleet'. At first sight this suggests a possibility of layings in Tollesbury Mell Creek or Mill Fleet, but the qualification reduces the description to an enigma.

The Wiseman brothers of Paglesham, Frederick 'late of West Mersea', and James, also had some ground in North Fleet or Salcott Creek, which they disposed of in 1888 to William Pullen of West Mersea for £130.

2 Philpots, J.: *op. cit.*

3 *Essex Standard*, 16 May 1846 and 19 July 1867.

Chapter 8

1 A dedicated student of the eighteenth- and nineteenth-century history of Mersea Island and a founder-member of West Mersea Yacht Club, he was found dead in his Mersea home in 1938 at the age of over 80 years.

2 *Essex County Standard*, 31 March 1967.

3 *Essex County Standard*, 7 November 1969.

4 French family papers in possession of Mr. Peter French, West Mersea.

5 From the corner of the sea wall down to just below the Dabchick's Sailing Club these were Cassell French, Peter French, George Stoker, Robert Stoker, Banks Bros. and Mrs. A. J. Hempstead.

6 A. J. Carter, S. French, A. French and Robert Stoker, who also owned Cobmarsh Island.

7 A. W. Mussett.

8 Owners R. Pullen, Ron Pullen, D. Mussett, Hector Stoker, Edward Woolf, Peter Vince, Savoy Hotel Group/D. Mussett, Clifford Mussett (dec.), Albert Clarke and Fred Bentley Ltd.

9 I adhere to the name Buzzen, as always pronounced, rather than the Ordnance Survey Besom, which I take to be the despairing effort of a surveyor to make sense of local lingo. Michael Frost of Colchester has suggested as a derivation of 'Bussand', the creek where the 'busses' or smacks lay, on the analogy of the corruption of the Ray Sand Channel into 'Rays'n'.

10 The existence of layings in the south end of the present Mersea Fleet, between Cobmarsh and Packing March islands, does not support the theory that this creek is of relatively recent origin, subsequent to the medieval inception of manorial leases. On the other hand, it seems not unreasonable to assume that if the Fleet did change its course from the west to the east side of what is now Packing Marsh, the layings may also have been transferred from the old channel to the new.

11 Including Joannes Janson, Amsterdam (1576), John Norden (1594), John Speed (1610), Joannes Blaeu (1645), William Kip (1653), Pet and Valk (1659), Richard Blome (1673), John Ogilby and William Morgan (1678), Morden (1695), John Oliver (1696) and Chapman and André (1777). The first maps showing two channels, i.e. Mersea Fleet and Thornfleet, are Emanuel Bowen's (1781), Carrington Bowles' (1781) and John Harrison's (1787). The two last mentioned are also the first to show Cobmarsh Island.

12 Vaudrey scrapbook in French family papers.

13 Manuscript record book in possession of Mrs. C. van Hood.

14 The other Wivenhoe owner was Frederick Nicholson, with twelve layings and two boats. At Brightlingsea John Tabor had twelve layings and three boats, Isaac Harwood nine and one, Anthony Tabor ten and one, John Jolly eight and two, John Tabor junior six and one, John Annis five and one, William Winterflood eight and one, Samuel Martin five and one and John Ellis two and one. At Tollesbury, C. Spurgeon had nine layings and one boat, James Bowles six and one and John Barrington five and one.

15 T. Overall had 18 layings and two boats, William Haward 15 (? hole in paper) and two. Steven Overall 16 and two, Samuel Overall seven and one, William Brand eight and one, John Brand four and one, John Barrett five and one, Bennet Hawes 15 and one, William Haward junior nine and two, Uriah Clarke four and one, J. Simpson three and one and F. Lucking two and one. William Haward's papers, 1791-1826, along with details of the building of the family's last oyster smack, *Evergreen*, in 1886, are in the Essex Record Office. William Overall's estate, including three or four layings and two smacks, was sold 'for the benefit of creditors' in 1822 and two years later the *Colchester Gazette* refers to 'Mr. Overall of Mersea, unfortunately drowned'.

Chapter 9

1 Bride, N. N.: *Old Leigh* (1954).

2 Essex Record Office.

3 Morant, Philip: *History of Colchester* (1748).

4 Berridge, Jesse: 'The common-place book of Mr. John Lee', *Essex Review*, LII (1943).

5 White, Wm.: *History Gazetteer and Directory of County of Essex* (1863).

6 Mayhew, Henry: *London labour and the London poor* (1864).

7 Taylor, Silas and Dale, Sml.: *The History and antiquities of Harwich and Dovercourt* (1730).

8 *Ipswich Journal*, 10 March 1750 and the papers of a Harwich fishing family in the Essex Record Office.

9 *Essex Standard*, 21 Aug. and 11 Dec. 1863, 11 March 1864, 14 June 1867, 8 April 1870.

10 Bacon, Nathl., *op. cit.*

11 *Ipswich Journal*.

12 *Essex Standard*, 5 April 1870. For the stone-dredging trade see Benham, H.: *The Salvagers* (1890).

13 Bulstrode, *Local Government Board report on Cholera* (1896).

14 *East Anglian Daily Times*, 2 Jan. 1914, reporting an oyster poaching case at which Horace Cooke's son, Victor, gave evidence. Cooke's address then was 10, Market Lane, Ipswich. The Colne Fishery minutes also report a preference for Ipswich oysters in 1905, so the revival seems to have preceded Cooke's lease.

15 Wood, E.A.: *Thorpe-le-Soken* (1975).

16 See Benham, H.: *The Smugglers Century* (1986).

17 Bulstrode, *op. cit.* (1896).

Chapter 10

1 Dickin, *op. cit.*

2 Inventories of the properties of Brightlingsea Manor survive for 1826 and 1860.

In 1826 the 'oyster layings and edgings' totalled just over 26 acres and comprised 13 in 'creek', of which three exceeded one acre, occupied by J. Stammers, E. Layzell and S. & J. Woovett; 23 in 'Flag Channel or Boar Fleet', including the School Laying, with only one over one acre (L. Everitt), and 12 edges in 'St. Osyth Channel or Cock Fleet', all measuring one rod, four perches. The edges on the other side of this creek presumably belonged to the Manor of St. Osyth. A separate section lists half each of Brightlingsea Creek, up to the ships carpenter's yard; of Flag Channel, north and south sides, to the same point, of St. Osyth Channel to 'top of Cyndry' and above this to Thorrington Bar, and of 'Ford Creek'. Rents from 44 occupiers ranged from ten shillings to £3; only a few had more than one laying.

The 1860 inventory lists, 'tenure by agreement', two layings in Brightlingsea Creek, 18 in 'Boar Fleet', and 11 in 'Cock Fleet'. Rents of these were up to £10, with many over £5. These were presumably enfranchised. A separate list shows eight leasehold and seven copyhold layings in Brightlingsea Creek (with one shown half-leasehold, half copyhold), bringing in a total rent of £17 at an average of £1 each. Fifty-five tenants of oyster pits paid £7. 10s.

3 Report to Fishmongers' Company.

4 Essex Almanac (Chelmsford).

5 Burgess Everett: 'The Technique of an oyster cleansing station', *British Fisheries Manual and Directory* (1947).

6 Aldous launched the *Guide* (8 tons), *Violet* (7), *Shamrock* (18), *Snowdrop* (12), *Miranda* (25), *Moss Rose* (27) and *Edith Francis* (11); Roots and Draper turned out *Jenny* (18), *Lily* (8), *Gordon* (22), *Fox*, *Essex Chief* (21), *Ann Sophia* (25), *Waterlily* (18) and *Lizzie Maud* (16); James built *Friendship* (18), *Blanche* (18) and *Waterwitch*. Besides these others were lengthened and converted to ketch rig and many were fitted with wells for the deep sea trade. The purchases included the *General Havelock* from Grimsby, *Ann Martins* from Ramsgate, *Topaz* from Dover and *Gipsy Queen* from Beaumaris.

Chapter 11

1 Oyster petition, quoted by Dickin, *op. cit.*

2 Maldon Corporation plea to Lord Mayor of London. *The Times,* 3 June 1837.

3 For the Colchester smacks, see Leather, John: *The Northseamen* (1971) and Benham, H. and Finch, R.: *Sailing craft of East Anglia* (1987). For the Harwich cod smacks which later joined the Brightlingsea fleet, see Benham, H.: *The Codbangers* (1979). For the Burnham boats, see Benham, H.: *The Smugglers' Century* (1986).

4 Brightlingsea Parish Magazine, Jan. 1884.

Chapter 12

1 *Suffolk Chronicle,* 29 June 1822.

2 See Benham, H.: *The Smugglers' Century* (1986).

3 Brightlingsea Parish Magazine.

4 Brightlingsea Parish Magazine.

5 In 1895 welled Grimsby smacks were bringing deep-sea oysters for re-laying at Cleethorpes, along with the American imports, on the grounds where natives had been dredged out, but I have not discovered how long this continued.

6 Frank Cock of Restronguet told me, 'My father said to me "I see the first of them in the harbour yesterday – C bloody K all over the sail. Now we'll have to lock everything up and keep an eye open all night". I still hate all Essex men for thieves and pirates', my old friend observed genially, 'all saving your dear good self, that is'.

7 Leather, John: *The Northseamen* (1971) and Board of Trade Report, 1876, quoted by Philpots: *op. cit.*

8 Including Joe Kirby and Ben Frost.

9 In 1864 130 boats were employed at Newhaven and 140 at Shoreham in the oyster trade. The discovery of new oyster grounds off Shoreham in 1849, 40 miles long and 10 miles wide, proved so irresistible to the Brightlingsea smacks that they missed that year's regatta.

10. Rudkin, D.J.: *The Emsworth oyster fleet* (1975) and Leather, John: *Gaff rig* (1971).

Chapter 13

1 Salmon, Nathaniel: *The history and antiquities of Essex.* (1740) (under Fingringhoe).

2 The commonplace book of Mr. John Lee: *Essex Review,* Vol. LII (1943).

3 Perhaps the Deputy, a Cinque Port title. Brightlingsea not being a Borough did not have a Mayor till the local goverment reforms of 1974 permitted half the parish councils in the country to adopt the office.

4 MS in author's collection 'copied from a manuscript book in the possession of Samuel Randall, Esq.' and dated August 1861. It includes references to reports in the *Ipswich Journal*, 20 Aug. 1791 (which gives no further details) and in the *Whitehall Evening Gazette*, 12 Nov. 1791 and the *St. James's Chronicle*, 20 Aug. 1791. An Act of 1581 gave Orford men the right to dredge up the Alde as far as Slaughden, though it is not clear if this was 'prescriptive' or 'exclusive', a matter which must have concerned Aldeburgh. In 1650 the Corporation appointed a Water Bailiff with an official measure to regulate the size of oysters, then priced at a shilling per hundred. The Fishery, advertised for lease in 1853 (*Essex Standard*, Jan.) but described by Bulstrode as 'abandoned' in 1894, continued till it was destroyed by the mortality of the 1920s and closed in 1930. The layings of Brittany and Portuguese oysters was revived in the Butley River by Richard Pinney in 1958, and its trade continues to the present.

5 Clarke, G.: 'A legal pearl', *Essex Countryside*, Nov. 1985.

6 *Morning Chronicle*, 30 Jan. 1808, quoted in *Essex County Standard*, 13 June 1908.

7 *Essex County Standard*, 4 March and 23 June 1894.

Chapter 14

1 Cromwell, T.: *History and description of the ancient town of Colchester* (1825).

2 Mills v. the Mayor, Aldermen and Burgesses of Colchester; *Essex Standard*, 12 Feb. and 18 Nov. 1864.

3 *The Colne Oyster Fishery: notes on its management* (1914): Colchester and Essex Museum. I have omitted shillings and pence from some figures for brevity.

4 *The Colchester Oyster Fishery* (1916). Laver's journal and a file of personal papers are also in the Essex Record Office's Colchester and N. E. Essex Branch (Accns. C133 and C235).

5 *Essex County Standard*, 2 March 1907.

6 Evidence at 1883 Blackwater inquiry.

7 Borough Treasurer: Summary of financial results.

8 Others included the *A. W. Hayward*, dumped there in 1909, the *First Fruits* in 1914, the *Iris* in 1938 and the Corporation's bucket dredger and M. V. *Crocus* in 1950 and 1953.

9 In 1913 two Colchester engineering firms were building internal combustion engines. The Britannia chosen was the product of the Britannia Engineering Co., which later became part of Paxman's. Mumford's could also offer 50 h.p. and 40 h.p. paraffin engines, fitted in Admiralty launches.

10 *Alert* and *Brisk* were built by Houston for £80. *Viking* was built by W. A. White & Son and cost £429. *Edward VII* was built by Forrestt & Co. at a cost of £1,307. She was 41ft. x 10ft., with double skin teak planking and an engine by Mumford of Colchester. She had a lavatory and wash basin – more probably for the members of the Watch Committee and Fishery Board than the convenience of the crew. The 20ft. *Raven* was built in 1892, and a 26-footer, probably *Colne*, in 1895. *Victoria* replaced *Alert* in 1897 and *Alexandra* replaced *Raven* in 1901.

Prince of Wales was built in 1901 by Aldous for £210. She was fitted with an engine in 1936, by which time the police also used a motor launch *Stella*. Other details, including plans of *Edward VII*, are in a file of police papers in Colchester Public Library. The police regatta is from *Colchester Gazette*, 19 August, 1896. Some yarns about the river police will be found in my *Last Stronghold of Sail*.

Chapter 15

1 *Essex Standard,* 14 June and 19 July 1867.

2 *Essex Standard,* 5 and 19 March 1875.

3 In view of his later associations with the Company, it is interesting to find Dr. Salter noting in his diary: 'gave evidence at the Blackwater Oyster Fishery inquiry, and stood a good bally-ragging for half an hour or so, doing the dredgermen some good I think'. Salter, John, H.: *Diary and reminiscences* (Bodley Head, 1933).

4 *Essex Standard,* 12 Oct. 1877.

5 *Essex Standard,* 6 Jan. 1883.

6 Brightlingsea Parish magazine, July 1882.

Chapter 16

1 French, Leslie: *Schoolday memories of West Mersea* (privately printed and undated).

2 While it has no direct bearing on the oyster story, it may be of interest to record that the re-establishment of the Mersea Herring Fishery, remembered by only the oldest fishermen, was one of my earliest collaborations with Peter French. During the Second World War some Belgian refugee fishermen employed by Lewis Worsp of North Sea Canners Ltd. at Wivenhoe, were returning up the Colne when soldiers exercising on the swing bridge then carrying the railway over Alresford Creek, threw some hand grenades in the water, the explosions killing a large number of herring. The Belgians persuaded Mr. Worsp to get them a few Scotch deep-sea nets from Lowestoft, but could catch nothing with them, probably because they tried in deep water and (I believe) in daylight. Lewis Worsp later gave me a net, which I cut into three two-fathom strips; this little fleet of three nets, used with a 12-foot dinghy, seldom failed to produce a few hundred herring with an evening low water, and when I boasted to Peter that I had caught 500 on the previous night, he observed, "If you can catch 500, I know I can 5,000 which would be worth doing". The *Mersea Lass* was soon equipped with drift nets and pioneered a fishery which soon became the mainstay of the local inshore fishermen and remains so to this day. As both Peter and Major Gardner, Chairman of the T. & M., were members of the Kent and Essex Sea Fisheries Committee at the time of the row over the laid-up shipping, I need not add that relations became a trifle strained.

Afterword, by Peter French

Considerable time has elapsed since Hervey wrote this account of the Essex oyster world. Needless to say there have been some changes and I am glad they are for the better. The picture of the industry's future was a very gloomy one indeed when Hervey penned his final chapter. Since then the relaying of Ostrea Edulis in the West Mersea area has continued and increased somewhat. They have thrived and mortalities have been relatively light. This is due to the fact that marketing has taken place in the early part of the selling season and that unsold stock, (those too small for market) have not been held over for the next season but destroyed.

In addition, due no doubt to the restriction in the use of TBT in antifouling paint on the boats' bottoms, water quality – in that respect at least – has improved and some very successful cultivation of Gigas has been possible, particularly in the upper reaches of the Blackwater where they are now produced by the million. Indeed, the indications are that Gigas will in future be the most cultivated bivalve.

The threat of Bonamia is unfortunately still present, as tests prove, and he would be a very brave man who relaid Ostrea Edulis in the quantities we used to and at the densities that were usual before it struck.

There has also been a report that some small numbers of spat have been seen. If this is correct it is another indication that the ban on TBT was justified and worthwhile.

The current situation is therefore one of hope that with prudent management and care the industry will continue to make a contribution to the coastal economy and provide some employment for at least a few.

Index